ANC
EGYPT

Ancient Egypt Contents

First published in 1981, with a different cover design by Usborne Publishing Ltd. 83-85 Saffron Hill, London EC1N 8RN.

Copyright © 1981, 1992 Usborne Publishing Ltd.

The name Usborne and the device 🐝 are Trade Marks of Usborne Publishing Ltd.

All rights reserved. No part of this publication may be reproduced, stored in a retrieval system, or transmitted by any means, electronic, mechanical, photocopying, recording, or otherwise, without the prior permission of the publisher.

Printed in Italy.

The first part of this book is full of fascinating information and colourful pictures which will bring to life the world of the Ancient Egyptians. There are lots of scenes, like the one above of people working in the fields, which have been carefully reconstructed from archaeological evidence.

Sometimes, instead of a reconstructed scene, you will see a reproduction of an Egyptian painting or carving – like this one of musicians playing. You will usually be able to recognize these by the flat way in which the figures are drawn. Also, the Egyptians always drew faces sideways on.

You will also find reproductions of models the Egyptians made and detailed pictures of things they used, such as furniture, jewellery, tools or weapons. Some are based on objects shown in Egyptian paintings or sculpture, but most of them show objects that have survived in tombs and still exist today.

The map on page 58 shows you where many of the places are that are mentioned in this part of the book.

Sometimes you will read about people other than Egyptians – Nubians or Syrians, for example. You can find out where they come from by looking at the map on page 4.

Your can find out more about the kings and queens mentioned in the book by looking at the "History of Ancient Egypt" on pages 59–61. Egypt's long history is divided into "Kingdoms" and "Periods", and you will come across these terms in the book. To find out more about them, see page 5.

You may want to visit a museum to see some Ancient Egyptian objects yourself. On page 62 there is a list of museums with good Egyptian collections.

Introduction to Ancient Egypt

The civilization of Ancient Egypt is one of the oldest in the world. It began more than 5,000 years ago and lasted for over 3,000 years. For a time Egypt was divided into two kingdoms – Upper and Lower Egypt. Then, in 3118BC*, the country was united and ruled by one king, called the pharaoh.

This book is mainly concerned with Egypt between 3118 and 30BC. During this time the Egyptians conquered many foreign lands and acquired an empire.

Thousands of years ago, the Sahara was green and fertile and inhabited by Stone Age hunters. Gradually the climate changed and the land became a desert. The hunters left to search for new land and settled in Egypt. There they learnt how to tame animals and plant seeds and became farmers. People may also have come from the south and east.

The Ancient Egyptians were descended from these early hunters. At the peak of their civilization they · produced great works of art, such as this mask of King Tutankhamun. Religion and the idea of life after death played a very important part in their lives.

In 30BC the Romans invaded. Egypt became a province of the Roman Empire and ceased to be an independent nation.

4   *3118BC means 3118 years before Christ.

Later the Egyptians became Christians, and then Muslims, and the ancient temples and palaces were buried in the sand and forgotten. In the 18th century, European travellers became interested in the ruins and then professional archaeologists began to dig. The hot, dry climate had helped to preserve things.

Much of what we know about the Egyptians comes from tombs. They believed the afterlife would be like life on earth, so they put in their tombs the things they thought they would need, such as food and furniture.

They painted the insides of the tombs with scenes from daily life, such as grape picking. These pictures tell us a lot about their lives. Also found in tombs were models which show people doing things and scrolls with writing on them. Some of it was a kind of picture writing we call hieroglyphics.

At that time, nobody knew how to read hieroglyphics. However, in 1799, a clue was found. A stone was dug up in the Nile Delta with three kinds of writing on it – Greek and two kinds of Egyptian, including hieroglyphics. A French scholar called Champollion worked out the meaning of one word by comparing the Greek with the hieroglyphs. From this word he was able to break the code and the Egyptian scrolls and inscriptions could be read.

This chart shows you the terms that are used for the different periods of Egyptian history. The important periods are the Old, Middle and New Kingdoms. The kings have been divided into "Dynasties", which are families or branches of families. This was done in the 3rd century BC, by an Egyptian priest called Manetho, who wrote a history of Ancient Egypt.

Period	Date	Dynasties
Predynastic	–3118BC	
Archaic	3118–2686BC	1&2
Old Kingdom	2686–2181BC	3–6
1st Intermediate Period	2181–2040BC	7–10
Middle Kingdom	2040–1786BC	11&12
2nd Intermediate Period	1786–1567BC	13–17
New Kingdom	1567–1085BC	18–20
3rd Intermediate Period	1085–664BC	21–25
Late Period	664–332BC	26–30
Ptolemaic Period	332–30BC	31

Life in the Country

Egypt is a hot, dry country with very little rain. Crops can only be grown in the lush, green fields along the banks of the River Nile, which was where nearly everyone lived.

The Ancient Egyptians pictured the Nile as a generous god called Hapy (shown here), who gave life and food to the land and the people.

Every July, the Nile flooded the land for a few weeks. This was called the "Inundation". The mud left behind made rich, fertile soil.

"Nilometres" were built to measure the height of the flood, so people could work out if there was enough water to provide a good harvest.

When there was not enough water for the crops, people starved. This carving shows people starving during a bad year.

To avoid the floods, the Egyptians built their villages on high ground or dug ditches round them to drain off the water.

To make use of the flood water, large canals were built, with a series of connecting channels and ditches to take the water to all parts of the fields.

Farmers controlled the flow of water to their crops by opening and closing the channels each day. It was a serious crime to try to cut off somebody else's supply.

The boundaries of the fields were marked with stones. Occasionally a dishonest farmer would try to steal some of his neighbour's land by moving the stones during the flood.

The king was in charge of making sure the vital water supply kept flowing. Here the king is opening a new canal.

People spent a few weeks every year working on the canals to keep them in good repair. This was part of a tax they owed to the king.

This figure is called a shabti. Shabtis were put in tombs to do the canal digging for the dead person in the afterlife.

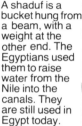
A shaduf is a bucket hung from a beam, with a weight at the other end. The Egyptians used them to raise water from the Nile into the canals. They are still used in Egypt today.

Water was carried from place to place in jars hanging from a yoke. These people are carrying water to water the lettuces in their vegetable garden.

A farmhouse

This house belongs to a wealthy farmer. We know what the houses looked like from pottery models, called "soul houses", which were put in people's tombs.

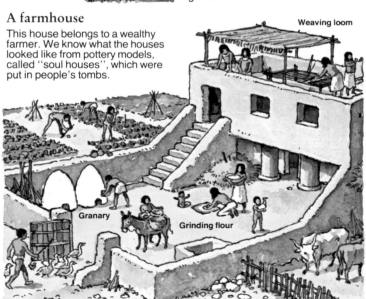

Weaving loom

Granary

Grinding flour

Sowing and Harvesting

In October, as the floods went down, farmers began to plough their fields. They used ploughs made of wood and bronze.

The main crops were wheat and barley. The seeds were sown by hand and animals were driven over the fields to tread them into the soil.

Animal skins filled with water were hung in the trees so that thirsty workers could refresh themselves.

As the crops grew, there was weeding and watering to be done and throwing stones to scare away the birds.

Then the taxman arrived. Here a worried farmer and his wife greet him with gifts, hoping for special treatment.

The taxman and his helpers measured the crops in the fields, to work out how much would be harvested and the amount that should be paid to the king in taxes.

Many things could go wrong before harvest time. The crop could be stolen or destroyed, but the farmer still had to pay the full amount of tax.

The harvest

The harvest was in March and April. Men cut the wheat using sickles with flint blades. People behind them gathered it together and loaded it into panniers, to be taken home on the backs of donkeys.

Women brought food and beer to the hungry harvesters. They also did the gleaning – collecting the wheat the men had missed.

Carvings in tombs show that musicians were hired to play to encourage the harvesters to work hard.

Offerings were put in the fields for the harvest goddess, Renenutet, who appeared as a snake to protect the grain.

In order to thresh the wheat (separate the grain from the straw), it was trampled on by cattle, which were driven round and round an area called a threshing floor.

To separate the grain from the chaff (its outer cover), women tossed it into the air, so the light chaff blew away. This process is called "winnowing".

Most people couldn't write, so scribes* were employed to record how well the harvest was going and what the yield was.

Granaries were for storing grain. The grain was poured through a hole in the roof and taken out through doors at the bottom.

The Egyptians did not use money, so farmers gave some of their crops or animals as taxes to the king.

Anyone who did not pay his taxes would be beaten as a punishment.

When the floods came, many people went off to work for the king. This was another way of paying tax.

Houses

The earliest houses archaeologists have found in Egypt were round huts made of reeds.

By the Middle Kingdom houses were built of sun-dried mud bricks and were rectangular. This model is from the 1st Intermediate Period.

This is a painting of a New Kingdom house. It looks a bit strange because the Egyptians didn't use perspective in their drawing.

A villa at Tell el Amarna

Many Ancient Egyptian sites have towns built on them now, so it is difficult to find houses to excavate. Amarna is an exception as no-one lives there now. This is a rich man's villa built in the New Kingdom. It is made of mud brick with a wooden roof and columns. It has a second storey which covers only part of the building. The front and centre of the house are used for conducting business and entertaining friends. The back of the house is where the family sleeps. Sometimes in the summer they sleep on the roof.

Stables

Kit

Rich people had bathrooms and lavatories in their houses. The walls were lined with stone to stop water splashing the bricks.

Often the walls were painted bright colours or had mats hung on them. This is part of a painted leather wall-hanging.

This is part of the painted mud floor of a villa. The rich sometimes had floors covered with glazed tiles.

Servants' quarters

Granaries for storing grain

Windows – they are small and high because of the heat.

Furniture

Most Egyptian houses had less furniture than ours. It was usually made from plain wood and reed, but rich people had furniture made from rare woods, inlaid with ivory or semi-precious stones and covered with gold. Some furniture had designs on it of flowers, animals or hieroglyphs.*

Thrones

These are the thrones of Queen Hetepheres (left) and King Tutankhamun (right). They are made of wood and covered with real gold.

Chairs

Most chairs had short legs and no arms. The legs were often carved to look like animals' legs.

Stools and cushions

Many people had stools, rather than chairs, or sat on cushions on the floor.

Inside a scribe's house

This is what it would have looked like inside the house of a scribe, who would have been fairly rich. The furniture is well-made but doesn't have the decorated inlays that a king's or noble's furniture would have had. There are mats, and curtains on the door made of reeds.

*To find out about hieroglyphs, see page 52

A princess's bedroom

The bed is made up with linen sheets. There is a wooden head-rest on the bed, which the Egyptians used instead of a pillow. The princess's clothes, wigs, jewels and make-up are all kept in boxes, inlaid with gold, ivory, semi-precious stones or faience – a substance rather like glazed china. The floors and walls are painted.

Chests and boxes

Chests, boxes and baskets of various shapes and sizes were common in every household. People used them for storing clothes and other things, as there were no cupboards.

Lamps

For lights, the Egyptians used lamps, which burned linseed oil. They varied from simple clay (left) to alabaster (right).

Tables

Tables, like chairs, usually had quite short legs.

Pot stands

Many Egyptian pots and jars had rounded or pointed bases. Stands made of wood or clay were used to keep them upright.

13

Clothes

The clothes of the Ancient Egyptians were made of linen, which comes from a plant called flax. In winter though, some people wore wool. Although fashions changed among the rich, most people's clothes remained much the same throughout the whole period.

A man wore a short kilt and a woman wore an ankle length tunic with two shoulder straps.

For much of the year it was very hot, so children often did not wear clothes at all.

For heavy outdoor work men usually wore loincloths, and women wore short skirts.

Headcloths were sometimes worn, but most people went bare-headed.

In winter it could get quite cold, so people wrapped themselves in large cloaks.

Everyone wore sandals made of leather or reed. Some nobles' sandals were made in quite fancy styles.

Some clothes, such as this linen robe, have been found in tombs. The gloves came from Tutankhamun's tomb, but there are no paintings showing people wearing gloves.

Making cloth

The flax to make the cloth is grown in fields. First it was picked, then the stems were washed and separated.

Pieces of stem were twisted together into a long, strong thread. This process is called spinning.

To make the cloth, the threads were woven on a loom. This job was done by women.

14

Old Kingdom

These are the clothes that would have been worn by nobles in the Old Kingdom. The woman is wearing a dress of beads over a plain white dress. The man's kilt is partly pleated.

Young men preferred their kilts short. Elderly officials wore much longer ones.

Middle Kingdom

This is a Middle Kingdom official and his wife. She is wearing a dress with embroidery on it.

Materials

The clothes shown in tomb paintings are usually white, as white was thought to be pure. However, small pieces of cloth and statues have been found, which show that the Egyptians did use coloured and patterned materials.

New Kingdom

In the New Kingdom, the clothes worn by the rich became much more elaborate. Women wore finely pleated dresses and flowing cloaks. Men sometimes wore long robes over their kilts.

Feathers and sequins

Some statues show kings and queens wearing clothes made of feathers. This picture shows a section of one of the statues.

Lots of rosettes and sequins have been found in Tutankhamun's tomb. They were probably sewn on to clothes.

Hair and Make-up

Egyptian men and women, of all ages and social backgrounds, used make-up. They kept it in boxes or baskets, like these.

The rich had mirrors made from highly polished silver, with decorated wooden handles. Poorer people had mirrors made of copper instead.

Lip and eye paints were made from minerals which were finely ground into powder on a palette. The powder was stored in jars and then mixed with oil or water before use.

Make-up was painted on to the eyes and lips with fine brushes and sticks.

People painted their eyelids with a green or grey paint, called kohl. They shaped their eyebrows with tweezers.

Razors were used for shaving hair. Priests kept their heads and bodies shaved.

This statue of a dancer has tattoos on its legs and arms. Some mummies have been found with tattoos.

Perfume

This carving shows women gathering lilies for perfume. The Egyptians made a lot of perfume, from flowers and scented wood.

The flowers were then mixed with oil or fat and left in pots, until the oil had absorbed the scent.

Perfumed oils were rubbed into the skin, to stop it from drying in the hot Egyptian sun.

Hairstyles

As the climate was very hot, most men and women kept their hair short, especially if they had to work outdoors.

Nobles had longer hair or wore wigs. Some kept their hair straight, others had plaits or curls.

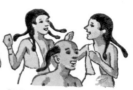

Children often had shaved heads with a single lock of hair. Young girls sometimes had several plaits.

The hairstyles of nobles varied according to the period. These are the styles worn in the Old Kingdom.

In the Middle Kingdom noblewomen sometimes wore their hair padded out and decorated with ornaments.

New Kingdom styles were very elaborate. For special occasions nobles wore heavy wigs with a lot of plaits and curls.

Wigs and combs have been found in tombs. The wigs were made of wool or real hair.

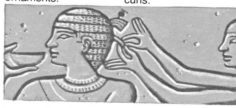

Instead of a full wig, some women added individual locks of false hair to their own. This carving shows a maid attaching a lock to her mistress's hair.

Both men and women wore perfume. They kept it in flasks like these.

This painting of a banquet shows a servant putting cones of perfumed grease on the heads of the guests. As the grease melted, it ran down the face with a pleasant, cooling effect.

Jewellery

Egypt and Nubia had gold mines, so a lot of jewellery was made of gold. This is an ancient map of a mine.

After being mined, the gold was weighed at every stage to make sure none of it had been stolen.

Goldsmiths heated the gold until it melted. To keep the fire hot, they pumped bellows with their feet.

The melted gold was then poured into moulds, or left to set and hammered into shape when it was cold.

The Egyptians used semi-precious stones, such as turquoise, garnet and lapis lazuli. Here, stones are being threaded into a necklace.

There was a wide range of jewellery for both men and women, though tomb paintings always show people wearing the same styles.

Crowns and head-dresses

Head-dress

Diadem

Rich people often wore some sort of jewelled head-dress. Here is a princess's diadem and a head-dress that was worn in the New Kingdom.

These delicate diadems belonged to a 12th Dynasty princess.

Here is an elaborate head-dress, worn by one of the minor wives of King Tuthmosis III.

Gold headbands and hair ornaments, like these, were worn by many noblewomen.

Earrings

Earrings were fashionable in the New Kingdom. Men and women had pierced ears.

Rings

People of all classes wore rings. Some had seals on them, or charms, called amulets.

Necklaces

Pendants were made in all kinds of materials, from shell to silver, which was rare and more expensive than gold.

Strings of beads were very common, judging from the number that have been found in tombs.

This bead collar is typical of the kind worn in the New Kingdom. It was fastened by cords at the back of the neck.

Pectorals

A pectoral was a large piece of jewellery, made in the form of a picture. It was hung around the neck on a string of beads.

This vulture pectoral belonged to King Tutankhamun. The vulture represents the goddess Mut, who was supposed to protect the king.

The decoration on this pectoral includes a scarab beetle and the eye of the god Horus. They are amulets, or charms which were designed to ward off evil spirits.

Belts

These dancing girls are wearing belts made of beads, some of which are shaped like shells. The beads are hollow inside and contain grains of metal that jingle as they move.

Funerary jewels

Most people had their jewels buried with them. Some, like these pottery beads, were made specially to be put in a tomb.

Bracelets and armlets

Men and women both wore bracelets and armlets. They could be a single string of beads, or a broad band of metal or beads.

Anklets

A lot of Egyptian women wore anklets, except when they were working.

19

Food

The Egyptians grew grapes for eating as a fruit and for making wine. They were grown on trellises like this.

Baboons were sometimes trained to pick figs for their owners, though the ones in this painting seem to be eating the fruit themselves.

Here are some of the fruit and vegetables grown in Ancient Egypt – cucumbers, peas, lettuces, onions, garlic, dates and pomegranates.

The Egyptians used honey to sweeten their food. Bees were kept in pottery jars.

The god Min looked after crops and animals. This carving shows the king making an offering to him.

Birds

Most farmers kept geese and ducks. This painting of geese is from an Old Kingdom tomb.

On some large farms, birds, such as pigeons and storks, were raised in aviaries and fattened for eating.

Catching wild fowl

The reeds along the River Nile teemed with wild ducks and other water birds. Fowlers trapped the birds with huge nets and sold them at the market. They were caught for eating, not just as a sport.

Animals

There was little land for grazing, as most fertile land was needed for growing crops. Egyptian cows were small.

When the floods came, herdsmen had to lead their cattle to the safety of higher ground.

A lot of cows were kept for milking. As milk goes sour quickly in hot climates, most of it was made into cheese.

Only rich people could afford to eat a lot of beef. Cattle for eating were kept in sheds and specially fattened up.

Sheep were raised for mutton. There were two kinds of sheep – one had horizontal horns, the other, curled ones.

The Egyptians kept goats for their milk and meat.

Pigs were kept, though they were associated with the wicked god, Set, so priests never ate pork.

For a time, people tried keeping hyenas to eat, but soon gave it up. The hyenas were probably too dangerous or too tough to eat.

The painting shows produce from the desert. Animals, such as deer, were hunted for meat; ostriches, for their eggs and feathers.

Fishing

The Egyptians ate a lot of fish. Fishermen usually went out in boats with huge nets. Sometimes two boats drifted side by side with a net between them. Some fishermen fished on their own, catching fish from the bank, using small nets or lines and hooks.

Cooking

Here are some butchers at work. Cattle were roped and pulled on to their sides to be slaughtered. The meat was then cut into joints and hung, ready to be eaten.

The Egyptians ate both wild and domesticated birds. After their necks were wrung, the birds were plucked and cleaned.

Here, fish are being gutted and cleaned. Sometimes fish was cooked and eaten immediately, but it could also be dried and stored.

Here is an Egyptian whisk and strainer made of reeds. Sometimes cooking utensils were put in tombs, to be used in the afterlife.

Most cooking was done outdoors away from the house, to avoid the danger of it catching fire. Sticks and dried grass were used as fuel.

To start the fire, a bow string was twisted round a stick and rubbed hard until it produced sparks.

Meat was often grilled over a brazier like this. A fan was used to keep the fire burning properly.

Making bread

Bread was an important part of the Egyptians' diet. Flour was made by grinding wheat or barley between two stones.

The flour was then mixed with water to make dough. Sometimes a flavouring was added, such as honey or garlic.

The dough was left to rise and then put into clay moulds, or patted into shape, and baked in a mud brick oven.

Beer and Wine

Egyptian beer was made from barley. The barley was put into jars full of water and left to stand.

Then lightly baked bread was crumbled into the jars and the mixture was left to ferment.

The result was very thick and lumpy, so it had to be stirred and then passed through a sieve.

The beer was then poured into jars. A covering, possibly a leaf, was placed over the mouth of the jar, with a lump of mud on top as a stopper.

The beer in the jars was still a bit thick, so it was usually poured through a pottery strainer before being drunk.

Making wine

To make wine, the grapes were put into a large trough and men trampled up and down on them. The juice that came out was used to make the best wine.

The last drops of juice were squeezed from the grapes like this. The wine made from this juice was of a poorer quality.

The juice was poured into jars and left to ferment. Then the jars were sealed and labelled with the date and the name of the vineyard.

Sports

Wrestling was a popular sport. One tomb painting shows details of many of the holds and throws that were used.

Fencing may have begun as a sport for soldiers. A wooden sword was used and a narrow shield fastened to the left arm.

Hunting hippopotamus and crocodile could be both exciting and dangerous. People went out in boats with harpoons and ropes.

Nobles went out hunting animals in the desert. This was done on foot until the New Kingdom, when horses and chariots were often used

Boatmen sometimes held water tournaments. The object was to push your opponents into the water with a pole, before they pushed you.

A day on the river

The Egyptians spent a lot of their free time on the river. Some just went for boat trips or picnics. Others tried to spear fish or catch birds by throwing sticks. Noblemen often had hunting cats, which were trained to find and bring back dead birds. Sometimes tame birds were held in the air to attract the other birds.

24

Children's Toys and Games

Brightly coloured leather balls have been found in the remains of Ancient Egyptian houses.

This Middle Kingdom tomb painting shows girls playing a game which involves throwing balls, while riding piggyback.

These children are playing a game rather like a tug of war. An Old Kingdom tomb painting shows several other, similar, energetic games.

Children played with spinning tops. A number of tops have been found in tombs.

Model animals made of mud, like these, may have been part of a farmyard game.

This ivory dog opens its mouth as if it were barking, when you press the lever in its chest.

By operating a handle at the side, you can make these ivory dwarfs twirl and dance.

Some dolls were made of wood and had moveable arms and legs.

This lion on wheels snaps its jaw as it moves along.

This basket containing a child's jewellery and charms was found in a little girl's grave.

25

Entertainments

Music was one of the most important forms of entertainment in Ancient Egypt. Professional singers and dancers performed in public during festivals and at private parties. No music was ever written down, though we know the words of some of the songs.

This tomb painting shows a typical group of musicians, with pipes, a lute and a harp.

Egyptian instruments also included flutes and lyres. Some, like this lyre, have survived in tombs.

Some noble households employed choirs of professional singers as permanent staff.

Most rich people were taught some musical skills as children. This noblewoman is playing to her husband.

As there was no written music, blind people, like this harpist, could easily become singers or musicians.

Dancing

Women dancers performed in processions at festivals. Some played tambourines or castanets to keep the beat. Young girls began training as dancers from an early age.

Tomb paintings show different styles of dances. This one appears to have been slow and graceful.

Others, like this one, were more lively and involved spectacular high kicks.

Some dancers hired for parties could also do acrobatics. This girl is turning a somersault.

The Egyptians probably enjoyed novelty acts too. This foreign slave girl is performing a dance from her country.

Indoor games

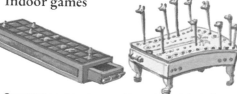

Senet was a popular board game, played rather like draughts.

Hounds and Jackals was probably also common, though we do not know how it was played.

Instead of dice, the Egyptians threw sticks or dried bones to decide how many moves could be made in a game.

An Egyptian party

Egyptian nobles had large parties with lots of food and drink. People often brought their pets – cats, dogs, monkeys and even geese. Singers, dancers, jugglers and acrobats were employed to entertain the guests. Servants served food and wine and offered people garlands of flowers and cones of perfumed grease to put on their heads.

Towns

Building land in towns was scarce, so many people lived in tall, narrow houses, several storeys high. They had no gardens, so they spent as much time as they could on their roofs, to catch the cool breeze. The streets were hot, dusty and noisy.

The market

Instead of shops, stalls were set up out of doors, selling locally produced fruit, vegetables and crafts.

Sometimes there was a stall selling beer, so that people could quench their thirsts in the heat.

Foreign Trade

Egypt was a great trading nation. Trade had been going on with neighbouring countries since Predynastic times. Although foreign trade was supposed to be controlled by the king, sailors would sometimes slip ashore to sell things privately.

From Syria and the Lebanon, Egypt imported wine, silver, slaves and horses. The Egyptians also imported Lebanese timber. This was important as few big trees grew in Egypt.

From the Nubian mines came an extra supply of gold for the Egyptians. They also imported Nubian copper, ivory, ostrich eggs and feathers, animal skins, amethysts, incense and slaves.

These people are Keftiu traders. They came from some islands in the Mediterranean Sea.

Wandering bedouin tribes came to Egypt from the desert to sell eye paints.

Cyprus exported copper, in pieces shaped like ox-hides, and opium, which was used as a medicine.

From Punt, which was somewhere in East Africa, the Egyptians brought back myrrh trees, which they used for making incense.

Here is an Egyptian boat being loaded with goods for export. The main exports were grain, papyrus, linen and rope.

People's Jobs

Most boys in Ancient Egypt followed the careers of their fathers. As soon as they were old enough, they followed their fathers into the fields or to a workshop where they learned a trade. Girls were generally expected to stay at home, helping their mothers, but there were some careers open to them. They could become musicians, dancers, professional mourners, weavers, bakers or midwives. They too began work at an early age.

Sculptors, carpenters, potters and other craftsmen usually worked together in workshops attached to a palace, temple or noble's house. There were a few who worked independently.

Potters

Egyptian potters mixed clay with finely chopped straw or sand, to bind it together. Men trampled up and down to mix it.

The pot was then shaped on a turntable, which the potter's assistant turned by hand.

The pots were baked in a wood-burning kiln. To prevent the pots from cracking, the fire had to be watched and the temperature kept even.

Carpenters

This is a set of carpenter's tools. They are made of copper and bronze with wooden handles.

Here are some carpenters at work. One man is polishing wood, the next is using a mallet and chisel. Another is shaping wood with a tool called an adze and the last is sawing.

Leatherworkers

Leather was used to make bags, sandals and many other things. These men are making arrow quivers.

Metalworkers

Here are some metalsmiths at work. Apprentices blow the fire to make it blaze fiercely. One man is pouring melted copper into a mould, while another is hammering a piece of cold copper into shape.

Royal tomb-builders

A good job to have in the New Kingdom was that of royal tomb-builder. The sixty men who worked on the royal tombs had their own village at Deir el Medineh, near the Valley of Kings. They were well treated, well paid and given plenty of free time.

There were slaves attached to the village to do the daily chores for them, such as chopping wood.

The men were divided into two teams, one for the right-hand side of the tomb, the other for the left. Each team had its own foreman.

Scribes kept a record of the progress of the work, the tools issued to workmen and the reasons for absence.

Wages were paid in goods, such as linen or food. Here a man is loading his wages on to a donkey.

We know from documents that sometimes the wages did not arrive and the men went on strike.

Boat-builders

Papyrus boats were made by tying bundles of reeds together. These boats were very light and were only used on the river, not on the sea.

To maked wooden boats, timbers were lashed and pegged together, so that, if necessary, they could be taken apart and rebuilt.

31

Temples

Along the banks of the Nile today you can see the remains of many temples. Most of them were built in the New Kingdom and later. Temples were dedicated to the worship of a particular god or goddess and contained a shrine with a statue, in which the god was supposed to live. Priests were in charge of looking after the god's daily needs.

The earliest temples, built in Predynastic times, were made of reeds and had flag-poles marking the entrance.

In the Old Kingdom, stone temples were built to honour the sun. A huge monument, a symbol of the sun god, stood in the courtyard.

This "kiosk" was built in the Middle Kingdom. This was where the god's shrine was taken during processions.

A New Kingdom temple

Temples were always built of stone and to the same basic design. They had an open courtyard, a hypostyle (pillared) hall and a holy of holies or sanctuary. People had to be specially purified before entering a temple. Only the king and priests could go beyond the courtyard.

Pylon or gateway

The capitals of the columns are shaped like plants

Obelisk (monument to the sun god)

Statue of the king

Sphinxes

A morning service

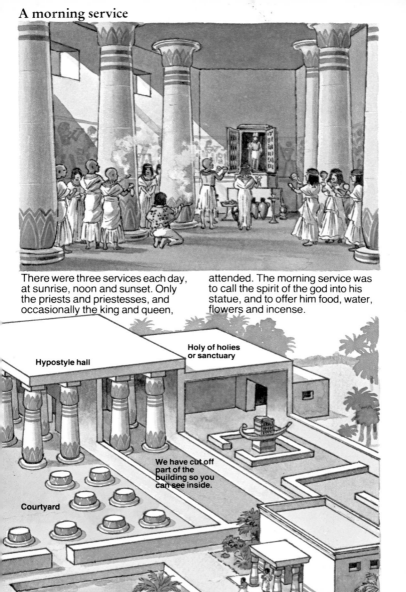

There were three services each day, at sunrise, noon and sunset. Only the priests and priestesses, and occasionally the king and queen, attended. The morning service was to call the spirit of the god into his statue, and to offer him food, water, flowers and incense.

Holy of holies or sanctuary

Hypostyle hall

We have cut off part of the building so you can see inside.

Courtyard

Sacred lake

Priest's house

Religion in Daily Life

Scarab beetle

Ankh – sign of life

Djed

Wedjet – eye of the god Horus

Amulets were charms which everyone kept to protect them from danger or evil. You can find them in the designs on jewellery or furniture. Here are some of the most common.

People used spells to protect themselves against illness, accidents or devils. Here a mother is holding an ankh and saying a spell to protect her child.

This wall has been cut away so you can see behind it.

The king could approach a god at any time to question him. This was called taking an oracle. In answer, the god might speak or raise an arm. In fact, a priest was hiding behind the statue, speaking or operating it, as he felt the god wanted him to.

Ordinary people could not enter temples, so they dictated their questions to the priest who read them for them.

Sometimes you could take an oracle from a sacred animal, representing a god. The priests prayed to bring the god's spirit into the animal and interpreted its reactions to give you your answer.

To win favour with the gods, people went on pilgrimages to temples, or to holy places, such as Abydos, where the god Osiris died.

Sometimes people gave carvings of ears on stone as offerings, to remind the gods to listen to their prayers.

Anyone who wanted to find out the meaning of a strange dream could go to a priest, who would consult his books.

If a prayer was answered or an illness cured, people usually left a gift at the temple to thank the god.

Festivals

During great festivals people stopped work and went out on to the streets. The statue of the god in its shrine was placed on a boat and carried on poles through the streets.

People could approach and ask a question or favour. If the answer was "yes", the statue would suddenly become so heavy that the bearers went down on their knees.

As part of the festival, masked priests and priestesses performed plays re-enacting the stories of the gods.

People took food and other offerings to the tombs of their dead relations, who were supposed to come through the false door to share the feast.

Illness

If you were ill, as a last resort, you could go to a temple for a cure. You spent the night in a room near the sanctuary.

The god might appear in a dream to cure you. If the god didn't come, the priest would try to cure you the next day.

Black magic

Evil people practised black magic. This woman is sticking pins into a model of a man hoping to kill him.

The King and Queen

The Egyptian king was called "pharaoh", which means "great house". Egypt had been ruled by two kings, one in the north (Lower Egypt) and one in the south (Upper Egypt). In 3118BC, the king of Upper Egypt conquered Lower Egypt and the country was united. The Egyptians believed their king was descended from the gods. He was High Priest of all the temples as well as head of the law and administration.

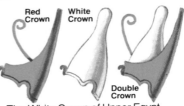

Red Crown   White Crown   Double Crown

The White Crown of Upper Egypt and the Red Crown of Lower Egypt were joined to make the Double Crown, worn by the king after unification.

On some carvings the unification of Egypt is shown by gods tying together papyrus and a lily – the symbols of the two lands.

The vulture goddess of the south and the snake goddess of the north are shown on the king's everyday head-dress.

Egyptians believed that at certain times the gods spoke through the king. This statue shows the king with the god Horus, shown as a falcon.

At the court

The king's daily duties included receiving advice and giving instructions to officials, architects and engineers, listening to petitions and receiving foreign ambassadors. Here a delegation of Libyans are paying their respects to the king and queen.

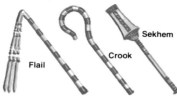

A sceptre is a symbol of a king's authority. In Egypt the most important were the Crook and Flail, but the king had others, such as the Sekhem (power) sceptre.

One of the king's roles was commander-in-chief of the army. New Kingdom kings were often great warriors and many led their troops into battle in person.

People paid taxes to the king in goods, such as grain, and services. The taxes paid for officials and workmen, and the care of the old and sick.

After a 30 year reign, a Heb Sed festival was held, to restore the king's health magically. During this, he ran along a special track.

Egyptians believed that when a king died he joined the god Osiris and ruled over the dead. This painting shows the king with Osiris.

The Queen

A king could have many wives but only one queen. She was usually the eldest daughter of the previous king and queen.

In the New Kingdom, the queen was also regarded as the wife of the god Amun. This made her the High Priestess.

If the king died while his eldest son was a child, the queen would become regent, ruling on behalf of the son.

Princes

In Ancient Egypt many children died young, so all the princes were trained carefully, in case they became king.

To become king, a prince had to marry the royal heiress, eldest daughter of the king and queen. This meant he had to marry his sister or half-sister. Here one of the minor wives is trying to introduce her son to the royal heiress.

37

The Government and Officials

The king governed with the help of his officials. These were often men who were related to the king, or who had been brought up with him. Others were ordinary men with distinguished careers in the army or as scribes in government service. The government was divided into departments of state – the Treasury, Foreign Affairs and Building. Each had a large staff, ranging from the chief official to the many scribes.

The most powerful official was the Vizier. His duties included reporting to the king each day on the state of the nation, giving orders to the various departments and collecting taxes.

Nomarchs, or governors, ruled the regions until the Middle Kingdom. Then they became too powerful and the king abolished them. This is the Nomarch Khnumhotep.

In the New Kingdom, a new official was created to govern the province of Nubia. He was called the "King's Son of Kush".

Some officials were sent on trading expeditions or put in charge of a mining project.

The king had a large staff of household servants and courtiers to attend on him.

The king's favourite courtiers and officials were called "fan bearers", after the emblem they carried. They always had easy access to the king.

If an official gave a beautiful daughter or sister to the king as a minor wife, this might win him favour.

A successful official could become wealthy, if the king honoured him with an award of gold.

Some people offered bribes to gain favours. Although officials were well paid, they sometimes accepted them.

Priests

Every temple had a High Priest and assistant priests of various ranks. To become priests, boys were trained in scripture and rituals. After a special ceremony, they were accepted into a particular temple, joining one of four groups of priests.

Each group was on duty in the temple for three months each year. Before going on duty, a priest had to be completely pure. His body was washed and shaved. He chewed natron – a kind of salt – and inhaled incense, to purify his mouth and thoughts.

All temples had priestesses too. Some could conduct religious services, but their main task was to sing hymns and make the responses to the prayers.

People paid taxes to the temple, to help support the priests. Sometimes disagreements arose over payment.

Priests were given different tasks. Some were in charge of the estates or workshops belonging to the temple.

Others specialized in performing funeral services or offering services to the dead.

Some priests studied the stars and the art of interpreting dreams.

"Wab" were men who never became full priests. They carried the shrine through the streets at festivals.

Musicians and dancers were attached to every temple and performed at most religious ceremonies.

Building

When the king wants to build a new temple the chief architect has to draw a plan and make a model for his approval.

Men begin quarrying stone from the cliffs. Using tools of stone, copper and wood, they drive lines of wooden wedges into the stone. Water is poured on to the wedges, to make them swell. As they swell, the slab of stone splits away from the rock face.

The stones are then dragged on sledges to the ships waiting to take them to the site of the new temple.

A lot of this work is done by men paying their labour tax to the king.

The king attends the foundation ceremony, in which the plan of the building is laid out with stakes and string.

The foundations are dug and the stone foundations are laid. Many of these workers are prisoners of war.

When the first layer of stone for the entire building has been laid, the areas between the stones are filled with sand.

A ramp of mud is built up alongside the first layer of stone, so that the second layer can be raised up more easily. After each layer of stone has been laid, the gap between the stones is filled with sand and the ramp made higher.

Once the roof has been completed, the ramps and sand are removed, so that you can get into the building.

Artists and sculptors

Before painting the wall of a tomb, Egyptian artists first made a grid of squares, to help them get the proportions of the drawing right. This was done with pieces of string soaked in paint.

Then a trainee artist drew in the required scene, taking care to follow the plan, which was drawn out on squares on a piece of papyrus. A master artist was there to supervise and make corrections.

Then the scenes were painted in, or carved and then painted.

Statues of gods, kings or private individuals were made for temples and tombs. The sculptors used tools made of copper and stone.
Sculptors and artists didn't sign their work.

Raising an obelisk

Sand
Ramps
Hole to remove sand

Obelisks, symbols of the sun god, stood outside temples. To erect an obelisk, ramps were built, with a hole in the middle filled with sand. The obelisk was pulled up the ramp backwards with ropes, then raised into position on top of the column of sand.

As the sand was removed from a hole in the bottom, the obelisk sank down slowly on to its base. Then the ramps were taken away.

Making mud bricks

Mud brick, rather than stone, was used for houses, palaces and government buildings. First large amounts of earth had to be dug.

The earth was mixed with water and straw, to help it bind together. This was done in a shallow pit by men stamping up and down.

When the mixture was ready, it was put into wooden moulds and left to dry in the sun.

The Army

In the Old Kingdom, men were drafted as soldiers by the local governors whenever they were needed. This system was abolished in the Middle Kingdom, as it had made the local governors too powerful and led to fighting between them. Gradually a royal army was built up. Some soldiers were full-time, others were drafted, probably as part of their tax duties to the king.

Until about 1600BC the army was made up of infantry, or foot soldiers, only. They carried spears, and shields of wood and leather.

Nubian archers were often hired to serve in the Egyptian army. Sometimes they had to fight in battles against their own people.

In the New Kingdom there were quite a few foreign recruits serving in special units of the army. They were people whose countries had been conquered by the Egyptians.

Fortresses

By the Middle Kingdom, the Egyptians had conquered part of Nubia. They built a chain of huge brick fortresses to protect this new southern frontier. Fortresses were also built along the eastern border, to keep out the bedouin tribes from the Sinai Desert.

Ships

The army used ships mainly for transporting troops. They fought very few sea battles.

Weapons

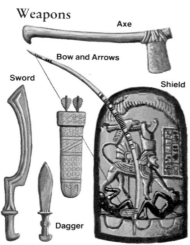

Here is a selection of Egyptian weapons. They were made of wood, stone, copper and bronze. Weapons belonging to kings or nobles often had rich inlays, like this shield belonging to Tutankhamun.

Sieges

For attacking enemy fortresses, the Egyptians had battering rams, with covers to protect the soldiers inside. Ladders were used to scale the walls. Some had wheels so that they could be pushed around.

Horses and chariots

In the New Kingdom there were four chariot squadrons in the army. Horses and chariots had been brought to Egypt by a people called the Hyksos, who conquered and ruled Egypt between 1670 and 1457BC. The chariots had two horses each and usually a driver as well as a warrior. Some soldiers did fight and drive, by tying the reins around their waists.

The Army on Campaign

In the New Kingdom the Egyptians believed that the god Amun directed the king to fight wars and conquer foreign lands. Here the king takes a sword from the statue of the god Amun.

This is a New Kingdom warrior ready for battle. His armour was made of leather, though it sometimes had metal scales. Some soldiers did other work during peacetime, so they had to be called up to fight.

On campaign the soldiers set up camps with tents. The officers had roomy, well-equipped tents with furniture, and servants.

This folding bed belonged to Tutankhamun. Officers probably had similar furniture in their tents.

There were four divisions in the army, each named after gods – Amun, Re, Ptah and Sutekh. These were subdivided into smaller units, with their own officers and battle standards. The standard bearer led the unit into battle.

Trumpets were used to sound orders on the battlefield. This trumpet, and the wooden stopper which fits inside when the trumpet is being transported, belonged to Tutankhamun.

As a reward for courage, a soldier could be awarded a golden "fly" by the king. Archaeological finds show that some people received several.

After the battle

After a battle the right hands of all the dead enemies were cut off, to find out how many had been killed.

Chiefs who had led rebellions were sometimes executed. Pictures show the king doing this himself.

Prisoners of war were paraded before the god Amun. They became slaves of the king, the soldiers, or the temples.

Many prisoners of war ended up in the mines or on building projects, though some became household slaves.

The children of conquered princes were taken as hostages, to make sure their families remained loyal.

In a peace treaty the king often took the daughter of a foreign prince as one of his lesser wives.

Conquered peoples

The conquered land became part of the Egyptian Empire and its people had to pay regular tribute to Egypt. Here are Syrians presenting gifts of gold vases.

Messengers travelled regularly to all parts of the empire with instructions from the king and greetings for foreign kings.

Once conquered, the Nubians adopted the Egyptian gods and way of life. New towns were built, and temples, like this one at Abu Simbel.

In the eastern part of the empire, Egypt installed garrisons, took taxes and controlled foreign policy, but did not try to change the way of life, as they had done in Nubia.

45

Law

The police force was probably made up of soldiers. In the New Kingdom, in Thebes, a Nubian tribe called the Medjay were used as police, and as guards for the royal tombs.

It was difficult for criminals to escape from Egypt, as they had to cross deserts and go without water. The police used dogs to follow their trail.

The law courts

Most criminals were tried in local courts by a group of judges, who were important local men. There do not seem to have been any lawyers, so people were expected to conduct their own cases.

Witnesses had to swear by Amun and the king to tell the truth. If they refused to give evidence or were found to be lying, they were beaten.

In very difficult cases, where the judges could not reach a decision, they sometimes appealed to the oracle for help.

Punishments included beating, the loss of an ear or nose and hard labour, but there were no regular punishments for particular crimes.

Scribes were always in court, to take down the facts and examine documents produced as evidence at the trial.

Documents have survived which tell us about some thieves who were caught robbing the royal tombs in the Valley of the Kings. They were given the death sentence.

Appeals could be heard by the king or the Great Court, where important trials were held. One such case was the trial of the minor wives who tried to kill King Ramesses III.

Marriage

With the exception of the king, very few Egyptian men had more than one wife at a time. The women of Ancient Egypt were in a much better position than most other women in the Ancient World. Although they had little political power, they had personal freedom and independence.

Many marriages were arranged, though surviving poems suggest that young people also made their own choices.

On marriage, a husband and wife set up a joint fund to provide security for themselves and their children.

All married women had property of their own, and were allowed to dispose of it as they wished, without consulting their husbands.

A woman could take charge of running her estate herself and would manage her husband's business when he was away.

If a married woman had a job, she could spend her wages as she liked and was responsible for her own debts. This woman is spending her earnings on expensive jewellery, much to the dismay of her husband.

A man who ill-treated his wife was usually looked down upon. He might be beaten up or taken to court by her family, or his wife might divorce him.

If a man divorced his wife, she kept her personal property, her share of the marriage fund and her children, and was free to remarry.

Here a dying woman is dictating her will to a scribe. Although the marriage fund automatically went to the children, she could decide who her own property should go to.

47

Funerals and the Afterlife

A nobleman has just died, although his family had hired the best doctors to try to save him.

The embalmers take the body to their workshops, where the internal organs are removed and put in "canopic" jars.

The body is covered with natron (a salt) to dry and preserve it and then wrapped in linen. We call an embalmed body a "mummy".

The heart is replaced with a magic "heart-scarab". Amulets are put in the bandages, to protect the body.

A mask is put on the head. Priests assist at the embalming, wearing masks to represent the gods.

After 70 days the funeral is held. The procession crosses the river to collect the body from the workshop.

The funeral procession

The procession, which includes professional mourners, priests and priestesses, then goes to the tomb. The coffin is drawn on a sledge. Servants carry furniture and offerings for the tomb. Egyptians believed life after death would be like life on earth, so they filled the tomb with everything the dead person would need for his comfort.

At the tomb door the "opening of the mouth" ceremony is held. This was supposed to give the dead man control over his body again. Then there is a funeral feast.

The coffin is placed in the stone sarcophagus in the underground burial chamber. The furniture and other offerings are put there too.

Then the priests leave, sweeping away their footprints as they go. The underground tomb chamber is tightly sealed, so that no-one can enter.

The rooms above ground are left unsealed, so that the Ka, or spirit priests, can come in and leave food offerings for the dead man.

The afterlife

The Egyptians believed that, during the ceremonies, the dead man's spirit crossed the River of Death into the Next World.

Having been given a Book of the Dead, containing a map and spells, he could pass through gates guarded by serpents.

He then had to be able to assure a group of stern judges that he had not committed various crimes while he was alive.

Before Osiris, the god of the dead, the man's heart was weighed against the Feather of Truth. If the heart was heavier, it meant he had led a wicked life and was handed over to a monster.

A good person entered a happy land, where all his dead friends and relations greeted him warmly.

Tombs

The earliest graves were holes in the sand, with stones piled on top. Ordinary people were buried like this throughout Egyptian times.

In Dynastic times, nobles and kings began to be buried in "mastabas" – mud brick buildings with rooms inside.

By the 4th Dynasty, stone mastabas were being used by nobles. Some had chapels attached to them.

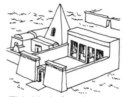

From the end of the Old Kingdom, nobles were also buried in tombs cut inside cliffs, which were decorated inside with scenes from daily life.

This kind of tomb was still being used in the New Kingdom, though some tombs, like the one above, had chapels with open courtyards.

This tomb is from the Late Period in Ancient Egypt. It looks rather like a very small temple.

Coffins

In early times, people who could afford it had wooden coffins. Other people were wrapped in mats.

An Old Kingdom noble was buried in a stone coffin called a sarcophagus. Some were decorated with carvings.

Many Middle Kingdom coffins were made of wood and brightly painted. They had "magic eyes" for the dead to see through.

Human-shaped coffins began to be used in the Middle Kingdom. The coffins were then placed in outer, rectangular coffins of wood or stone. This one belonged to King Tutankhamun.

This decorated wooden coffin and heavy stone sarcophagus come from the Late Period.

Pyramids and royal tombs

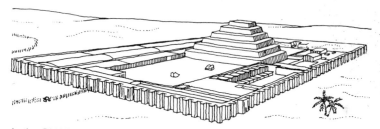

In the Old Kingdom, kings were buried in pyramids. the earliest ones are called "step" pyramids, as they were built in steps. The Egyptians believed that the king climbed up the pyramid to the stars. The first one, which is shown above, was built for King Zoser at Sakkara.

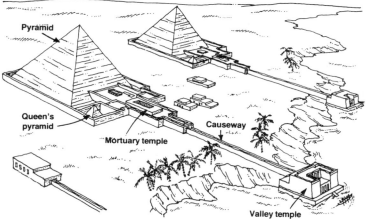

Pyramid

Queen's pyramid

Mortuary temple

Causeway

Valley temple

At the beginning of the 4th Dynasty, step pyramids were being replaced by "true" pyramids, like these. There was a collection of buildings around them. The embalming was done in the valley temple. Offerings to the dead king were made daily in the mortuary temple.

12th Dynasty pyramids were built of mud brick with a stone casing, instead of all stone. They lost their shape once the stone wore off.

In the New Kingdom, kings were buried in tombs cut into the rock in the Valley of Kings, at Thebes. Treasure was buried with them and the tombs were often attacked by robbers.

Writing

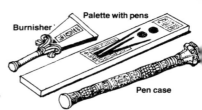

The Egyptians made written records of all business and legal matters, but as many people in Egypt could not read or write, scribes were specially employed to do this.

This is a scribe's writing equipment – a palette with pens, a pen case and a burnisher for smoothing down papyrus, a kind of paper made from papyrus reeds.

First the reeds were gathered and the outer green skin peeled away (left). The inner part was cut into strips and soaked in water (centre). Then the strips were placed, just overlapping, to make a sheet, with a layer of strips going the other way on top (right). The sheet was then pressed, dried and rolled.

Hieroglyphs

The Egyptians used a picture writing called hieroglyphs. At first, pictures were used just to represent objects. Later, the system developed and pictures and signs were used to represent sounds. Some sounds were for one letter, others were for groups of up to five letters. Words were built up of several different signs. Sometimes there was a picture of the object or action at the end of the word, to make it clearer what the word meant.

Hieroglyphs were always used on monuments, but there were two shorthand scripts invented for everyday use. The one shown above is called hieratic.

Some hieroglyphs

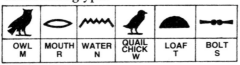

OWL M	MOUTH R	WATER N	QUAIL CHICK W	LOAF T	BOLT S

FLAX H	FACE HR	SANDAL STRAP ANKH	GOOSE SA	SWALLOW WR	BEETLE KHEPER

You can always recognize a king's name, as it is written in an oval frame, called a cartouche.

Education and Science

Most Egyptian children didn't go to school. Instead boys were taught a trade by their fathers, as soon as they were old enough, while girls helped their mothers. Those who could afford it sent their sons to school or employed private tutors. Girls from rich families were taught to write too.

At school the children were taught to read and write. They spent much of the day copying texts or doing dictations. Rich or clever pupils sometimes went on to study history, maths, religion, geography and languages too.

For notes and exercises, ostraca were used instead of papyrus. These were pieces of stone or broken pot.

Boys who had received a good education might become one of the king's officials. Languages were important for anyone dealing with foreign affairs or trade.

Science

Egyptian doctors were famous for their knowledge and skill. Surviving texts give details of medicines and treatments.

This papyrus sets out sums involving triangles. Texts like this show that Egyptian scholars were good mathematicians.

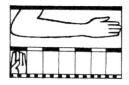

Their measurements were based on the body. Elbow to fingertip was one cubit. Seven hands, each four fingers wide, also equalled one cubit.

Egyptians studied the positions of the stars, which they named after animals and gods. This is a map of the skies.

10 days = 1 week
30 days = 1 month
4 months = 1 season
3 seasons = 1 year
360 days + 5 days = 1 year

This is the Egyptian calendar. Years were numbered from the beginning of the reign of each king.

Water hole

The day was divided into 24 hours. This is a water clock. You could tell the time by the water level as the water dripped through a hole.

Gods and Goddesses

Before Egypt was united, each region had its own gods and legends, so after the unification there were many gods – some local, some common to all Egypt. Most gods were associated with a particular animal, and they are often shown with the head or body of that animal. The Egyptians believed the gods ruled everything in nature, including the sun and sky.

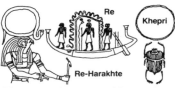

The sun god was one of the most important gods. The Egyptians had many versions of the sun god, but **Re** was the most common.

There were various stories about how the world began. One story is that it began with water. Then land appeared with a lotus flower on it. The flower opened and out of it came **Re**, who created the world.

In Memphis people said that their god **Ptah** created the world by saying the name of each thing, and so bringing it to life. His wife, **Sekhmet**, was goddess of war.

The body of the sky goddess, **Nut**, stretched from horizon to horizon. Her father **Shu**, god of air, stood over her brother **Geb**, god of earth, to hold her up.

In the New Kingdom, the god Amun was identified with Re and became **Amun-Re**, king of the gods.

Thoth was god of wisdom and scribes and helped judge the dead. Symbol: Ibis bird.

Maat. Goddess of truth. She kept the universe in harmony. Symbol: feather.

Khumn. Potter god who made babies. Symbol: ram.

Bast. Mother goddess, worshipped in the Late Period. Symbol: cat.

Sobek. God of water. Worshipped by many people because they feared him. Symbol: crocodile.

The story of Osiris

Osiris was the great-grandson of Re and god of the dead. He married his sister, the goddess **Isis**, and they became two of the most popular and influential gods. People believed they had once ruled Egypt, as king and queen. Here is a story associated with them.

Their brother **Set**, god of deserts, storms and war, was jealous. He murdered Osiris and cut his body into pieces.

The god **Horus**, son of Isis and Osiris, fought and defeated Set, who was diguised as a hippopotamus.

Anubis, the god of embalming, helped to collect the pieces of Osiris's body and bring him back to life.

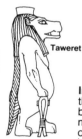

Horus's wife, **Hathor**, was goddess of music, dancing and happiness. She also cared for the dead. Symbol: cow.

Household gods

Some gods were not worshipped in temples, but by ordinary people in their houses. **Bes**, the dwarf, was god of marriage and children. **Taweret**, who is shown as a hippopotamus, was goddess of pregnant women.

Imhotep, architect of the first stone pyramid, became god of medicine. He was the only commoner ever to become a god.

Sacred animals

Some temples kept an animal, as it was believed that the god's spirit could enter into it. A bull, known as the **Apis bull**, was always kept in Memphis. It was seen as the spirit of Ptah and buried as a king.

In the Late Period, whole species of animals were worshipped and buried with honour. This is a mummified cat.

Travel and Transport

It was useless to build roads in Egypt, as they would have been covered and washed away by the floods every year. So instead, people nearly always travelled by boat, with the Nile as Egypt's highway. This affected the Egyptian way of looking at things. Their words for north and south were "downstream" and "upstream". They also believed there was a river like the Nile in the sky, and every day the sun god sailed in a boat from one side of the world to the other.

Foreign trading vessels

Local cargo boat

Noble in private boat on official business.

Local ferry taking people from one side of the river to the other.

The earliest boats were made of reeds. These were used on the river throughout Ancient Egyptian times. as there was a shortage of good timber for boat-building.

By about 3200BC, wooden boats were in use. The wood was imported from the Lebanon, which had excellent timber. All sea-going ships were made of wood.

All heavy cargo went by river. Obelisks were taken on barges from the quarries to the temples, towed by smaller boats. During the floods the river became wider, so boats could travel further inland.

This is a funeral barge, used by embalmers to carry corpses across the river to their workshops on the west bank.

The royal family travelled around on splendidly decorated ships. This is what the Royal Ship of Tutankhamun may have looked like.

Travel on land

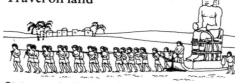

Statues and other heavy objects were pulled on sledges by teams of men with ropes. Water or oil was poured on the ground in front of the sledge, to help it run smoothly.

Traders used donkeys to transport things across the desert. Camels were not used until the Late Period.

To get around on land most people had to walk. Some very rich people were carried by their servants in chairs like these. Donkeys could be used for longer journeys.

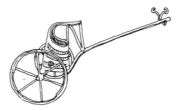

Once chariots had been introduced in Egypt, noblemen could travel much faster. However most people could not afford horses and chariots.

A Map of Ancient Egypt

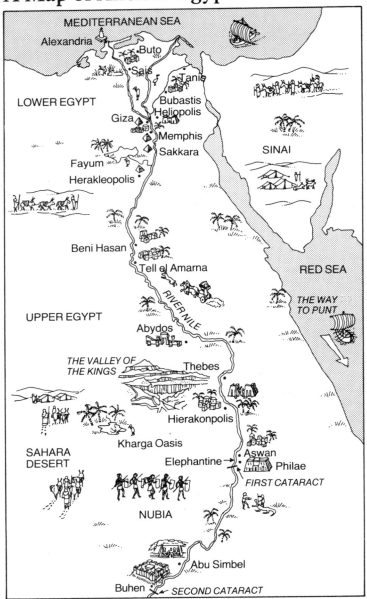

The History of Ancient Egypt

Thousands of years ago, Stone Age hunters lived in the Nile Valley. They have left behind remains, such as flint tools.

Predynastic Period

Later the hunters learned to tame animals and farm the land. The first farmers we know of were a group in Upper Egypt called Badarians. They made red pottery with black tops. Next came the Amratians, who made decorated pots, often with animal designs on them. After them were the Gerzeans. During this period, writing was invented and Egypt was divided into two kingdoms. These early cultures are named after the places where their remains were found.

Badarian pot

Amratian Pot

Gerzean Pot and Figure

Archaic Period

In 3118BC, Menes, King of Upper Egypt, conquered Lower Egypt and so united the country. He became the first king of United Egypt, and of the 1st Dynasty. A new capital city was built at Memphis and a graveyard at Sakkara.

Old Kingdom

The period known as the Old Kingdom began with the 3rd Dynasty. It was a time of peace and prosperity, with no invasions from abroad. This was the time when the great pyramids were build. The first was the "step" pyramid at Sakkara, designed by the architect Imhotep for King Zoser.

The pharaohs of the 4th Dynasty built their pyramids to a different design. They are called "true" pyramids and the most famous are at Giza.

It was an age of great achievement in art, especially sculpture. These statues are of Prince Rahotep and his wife, Nofret.

1st Intermediate Period

Then came a troubled period. The nobles grew more powerful and the pharaohs lost their influence. Wars took place between local governors wanting to gain power.

Middle Kingdom

The wars came to an end when Mentuhotep, a prince of Thebes, seized power and reunited the land. This second period of peace and prosperity is called the Middle Kingdom. A magnificent tomb was built for King Mentuhotep at Thebes.

The 12th Dynasty kings had a new capital city built near the Fayum, a marshy piece of land which they had drained. Northern Nubia was conquered and a chain of fortresses was built to protect Egypt's new southern frontier from attack.

A lot of beautiful jewellery, such as this princess's crown, was made in the Middle Kingdom.

2nd Intermediate Period

Royal power declined once again and the country was torn by civil war. Egypt was invaded from the east by a people called the Hyksos, who ruled the country for over a hundred years. They brought the horse and chariot to Egypt. Finally a prince of Thebes led a revolt and expelled them.

New Kingdom

The New Kingdom began after the expulsion of the Hyksos. During this period, the Egyptians conquered a vast empire, which they ruled from the new capital, Thebes. The dotted line on the map shows the furthest extent of their empire.

Between 1503 and 1482BC Egypt was ruled by a woman pharaoh, Queen Hatshepsut, who seized power at the death of her husband. She was succeeded by her nephew, Tuthmosis III (1504–1425). He was a great warrior and much of Egypt's empire was won during his reign.

A later king, Amenophis IV (1379–1362), decided to abolish all the gods except one, Aten, the sun's disc. He changed his name to Akhenaten and made everyone worship Aten. He and his wife, Nefertiti, had a new capital built, at Amarna.

These changes were unpopular, so the next king, Tutankhamun (1361–1352), brought back the old gods and moved the capital back to Thebes.

Egypt's enemies had grown stronger during Akhenaten's reign. Ramesses II (1304–1237) helped to restore the country's prestige. He was responsible for the building of the temple at Abu Simbel in Nubia.

Ramesses III (1198–1166) was Egypt's last great warrior king. He helped defend the country from invasion, by fighting a battle with a people from the Mediterranean islands, who were known as the "Sea Peoples".

3rd Intermediate Period

After this, Egypt began to decline. It was attacked by many invaders and many of the royal tombs were robbed. The empire was lost. For a hundred years a Nubian family ruled Egypt, as the 25th Dynasty. Then, in 664BC, Thebes was overrun by the Assyrians.

Late Period

In 664BC, the Prince of Sais drove out the Assyrians and later united Egypt under the 26th Dynasty. But in 525BC the Persians conquered Egypt and made it part of the Persian Empire.

The Persians were much hated and when Alexander the Great conquered Egypt in 332BC, he was welcomed by the Egyptians.

Ptolemaic Period

When Alexander died, his general, Ptolemy, founded a new dynasty of kings (the 31st and last), who ruled Egypt from the new city of Alexandria.

Roman Conquest

The last Ptolemy, Cleopatra, and her Roman husband, Mark Anthony, committed suicide after being defeated by the Romans. Egypt then became a Roman province.

Museums

Here are the names of museums where you can find exhibits from Ancient Egypt.

Australia

National Gallery of Victoria, **Melbourne**
Australian Museum, **Sydney**
Nicholson Museum of Australia, **Sydney**

Canada

Ethnological Museum, McGill University, **Montreal**
Museum of Fine Arts, **Montreal**
Royal Ontario Museum, **Toronto**

United Kingdom

City Museum, **Bristol**
Fitzwilliam Museum, **Cambridge**
Museum and Art Gallery, **Dundee**
Gulbenkian Museum of Oriental Art and Archaeology, **Durham**
Royal Scottish Museum, **Edinburgh**
Art Gallery and Museum, **Glasgow**
Burrell Collection, **Glasgow**
Hunterian Museum, **Glasgow**
Museum and Art Gallery, **Leicester**
Merseyside County Museum, **Liverpool**
School of Archaeology and Oriental Studies, **Liverpool**
British Museum, **London**
Horniman Museum, **London**
Victoria and Albert Museum, **London**
University Museum, **Manchester**
Castle Museum, **Norwich**
Ashmolean Museum, **Oxford**
Pitt Rivers Museum, **Oxford**

United States

Walters Art Gallery, **Baltimore,** Maryland
Robert H. Lowie Museum of Anthropology, **Berkeley,** California
Museum of Fine Arts, **Boston,** Massachusetts
Brooklyn Museum, **Brooklyn,** New York
Fogg Art Museum, Harvard University, **Cambridge,** Massachusetts
Semitic Museum, Harvard University, **Cambridge,** Massachusetts
Field Museum of Natural History, **Chicago,** Illinois
Oriental Institute Museum, **Chicago,** Illinois
Art Museum, **Cincinnati,** Ohio
Museum of Art, **Cleveland,** Ohio
Art Museum, **Denver,** Colorado
Detroit Institute of Arts, **Detroit,** Michigan
William Rockhill Nelson Gallery of Art, **Kansas City,** Missouri
County Museum of Art, **Los Angeles,** California
Institute of Arts Museum, **Minneapolis,** Minnesota
Yale University Art Gallery, **New Haven,** Connecticut
Metropolitan Museum of Art, **New York**
Stanford University Museum, **Palo Alto,** California
Pennsylvania University Museum, **Philadelphia,** Pennsylvania
Museum of Art, Carnegie Institute, **Pittsburgh,** Pennsylvania
University Art Museum, **Princeton,** New Jersey
Rhode Island School of Design, **Providence,** Rhode Island
Museum of Fine Arts, **Richmond,** Virginia
Art Museum, **St Louis,** Missouri
Museum of Man, **San Diego,** California
M.H. De Young Memorial Museum, **San Francisco,** California
Rosicrucian Museum, **San José,** California
Art Museum, **Seattle,** Washington
Museum of Art, **Toledo,** Ohio
Smithsonian Institution, **Washington D.C.**
Art Museum, **Worcester,** Massachusetts

Ancient Egypt Index

ANCIENT GREECE

Ancient Greece Contents

This part of the book tells you what life was like in Ancient Greece. There are lots of scenes, like this one of people at the theatre, which have been reconstructed from archaeological and written evidence.

Sometimes, instead of a reconstructed scene, you will see a reproduction of a Greek painting or carving. The paintings mostly come from Greek pots, which were often decorated with scenes from daily life.

There are also detailed illustrations of things the Greeks used, such as furniture, tools, jewellery and weapons. Some are based on objects shown in paintings or described in books, but most show things that can still be seen today.

The history of Ancient Greece is divided into "Ages" and "Periods". You can find out what these are in the chart on page 69. This part of the book concentrates on life in the Classical Period, although there are references to the Archaic and Hellenistic Periods too. For an outline of the history of Ancient Greece and its key personalities, see pages 124-125.

Greece in this period was divided into independent city states. This book concentrates on Athens, which was the largest and most powerful, although much of the information applies to the other states as well. Sparta is considered separately, as many customs there were different from the rest of Greece.

You may want to see some Ancient Greek objects and ruins for yourself. On page 126, there is a list of museums with good Greek collections, as well as sites in Greece.

The map on pages 122-123 shows you where many of the places are that are mentioned in this part of the book.

67

Introduction to Ancient Greece

The history of Greece can be traced back to Stone Age hunters. Later came early farmers and the civilizations of the Minoan and Mycenaean kings. This was followed by a period of wars and invasions, known as the Dark Ages. In about 1100BC, a people called the Dorians invaded from the north and spread down the west coast. In the period discussed in this book – about 500–336BC – Greece was divided into small city states, each of which consisted of a city and its surrounding countryside.

This map shows the main provinces and islands of Ancient Greece.

The land

Greece is a hot, dry, mountainous country. The hills were probably more wooded in ancient times than they are now. Good farming land was limited to narrow valleys and coastal plains. People were never far from the sea, so it played an important part in their lives. The Greek coastline is full of inlets and bays and there are many islands.

The people

In the Classical Period, most Greek city states had governments that were democratically elected by the citizens. Not all the inhabitants were citizens, however. Excluded from citizenship were all women, foreigners, slaves and freed slaves. Slaves were usually prisoners of war, or people born of slave parents.

A citizen and his wife

Foreigners

Slaves

How we know about the Ancient Greeks

Useful evidence can be drawn from ancient buildings. Some of these are still standing, although in ruins, others have been excavated by archaeologists. Carvings and paintings on buildings sometimes record historical events, as well as myths and legends.

The writings of Greek historians, philosophers, poets and playwrights have taught us a great deal about how people lived and thought.

Pottery is an important source of information. Changes in the shapes and designs help archaeologists to date the sites where pots are found and learn more about where the Greeks traded. Paintings on the pots tell us about their lives and their traditional stories.

Chart of main periods

c.*6000-2900BC	Neolithic Period
c.2900-2000BC	Early Bronze Age
c.2000-1400BC	Minoan Age (on the island of Crete)
c.1600-1100BC	Mycenaean Age (on mainland)
c.1100-750BC	The Dark Ages
c.750-500BC	Archaic Period
c.500-336BC	Classical Period
c.336-146BC	Hellenistic Period

*c. stands for circa, which means "about".

The City of Athens

Acropolis

Agora (marketplace)

The city of Athens dates back to Mycenaean times. It was built around the *acropolis* (meaning "high town"), the city's strongest point. The Athenians claimed that they were descended from the Ionians, who had lived in Greece before the coming of the Dorians. In the Classical Period, there were probably just over a quarter of a million people in Athens and the surrounding countryside. It was a wealthy city, partly due to the possession of rich silver mines at Laureum. These helped pay for the navy and foreign trade. There was a port at Piraeus, about 6km from Athens.

Fountain house

Law Courts

Council's meeting house

Odeion (small theatre)

Temple of Ares

Temple of Aphrodite

Houses

Part of this house has been cut away, so you can see inside.

Bedroom

Dining room

Altar

Herm

Greek houses were usually built from sun-dried mud bricks on a stone base. No complete houses have survived, but excavations give us an idea of the general layout. Houses were usually arranged around an open courtyard, which had an altar for family prayers. Many houses had an upper storey with bedrooms. The rooms at the front of the house were sometimes hired out to shopkeepers. At the front door there was a statue, called a *herm*, which was meant to guard the house.

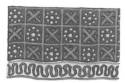

The walls inside were often plain, though lengths of patterned material may have been used as wall-hangings.

In rich people's houses the walls were sometimes painted with a patterned border. Later, whole walls were painted too.

By Hellenistic times, wealthy people had floors decorated with mosaics – pictures made from coloured stones or pebbles.

Some houses had a well in the courtyard, which meant that the house was supplied with as much water as was needed.

Most people, however, had to fetch their water from public fountains. This job was left to the women, although it involved carrying heavy jars. The public fountain was a place where women could meet each other and talk.

In Greek houses there were separate living quarters for men and women. The women spent much of their time spinning and weaving in the loom room.

In the kitchen, women ground grain into flour to make bread. There were pottery ovens for baking bread and charcoal fires for cooking meat and vegetables. The smoke escaped through a hole in the roof.

There were store rooms for keeping supplies of food, oil and wine. Wine was kept in storage jars, called *amphorae*.

Furniture

Most Greek furniture was made of wood and bronze. Although very little has survived, statues, carved stone reliefs and paintings on pots show us what it was like. Wealthy people had beautifully carved furniture, inlaid with gold, silver and ivory. Poorer people had plainer furniture.

Chairs and stools

A *thronos* was a special chair, usually made of marble. It was meant for an important official or a god.

Chairs like this one, with a back and arms, were reserved for the master of the house and honoured guests. They often had a footstool.

A *klismos* was a graceful chair with a curved back and legs. It had a seat of plaited leather and often a cushion on top.

Carvings and inlays on furniture showed designs of birds, animals, imaginary creatures, flowers and plants.

Most people sat on stools rather than chairs. A stool was called a *diphros*. Some had straight legs, others were curved. Some stools could be folded and carried.

Beds and couches

Couch

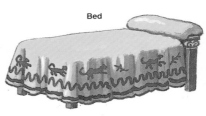

Bed

Beds and couches were both the same shape and had mattresses and pillows. Couches were used by men for reclining on, particularly at mealtimes. Beds had covers on them as well.

74

Chests, boxes and baskets

There were no cupboards, so people used chests and baskets for storing clothes, documents and other things. Many women had small caskets for keeping their jewels in.

As this carved relief shows, many things were simply hung on pegs on the wall.

Tables

Tables were usually low, so that they could be tucked under couches after meals. Most tables were oblong and often only had three legs. There were round and oval tables too.

Lamps

Greek houses were lit by oil-burning lamps, made of pottery or metal. There were special stands on which the lamps could be stood or hung.

Baths and basins

Very few houses had baths, so most people used basins instead. This painting shows someone preparing for a wash.

Clothes

The basic article of clothing for both men and women was the *chiton*, a tunic made from a rectangular piece of cloth. Men usually wore it just above the knee and women wore it full-length.

Women's clothes

There were two main styles of women's dresses – the Doric and the Ionic. The Doric *chiton* was usually made of wool. The cloth was folded in half lengthways and folded over at the top. It was fastened at the shoulder with brooches. Sometimes the side was sewn up.

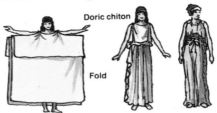

Doric chiton

Fold

The Ionic *chiton* was made of two pieces of cloth, usually linen, sewn up at the sides. It was left open at the top, but fastened together in several places. This style began being worn in Athens in the 6th century BC. Late in the Classical Period, silk and cotton were also being worn.

Ionic chiton

Dresses were sometimes worn with belts or binding across the chest.

Some materials were patterned or had patterned borders.

Cloaks and shawls

Light shawls were worn in a variety of different styles. Outdoors, women wrapped themselves in huge cloaks. They sometimes wore a hat too, to protect them from the sun.

Men's clothes

Men's tunics were made of wool or linen. They were fastened with a brooch at one or both shoulders and a belt was worn round the waist.

Although plain tunics were common, some tunics were patterned all over or had decorated borders.

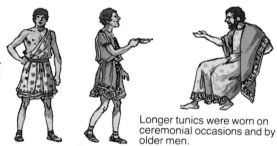

Longer tunics were worn on ceremonial occasions and by older men.

Cloaks

As their climate was so warm, the Greeks did not need many clothes. A large, rectangular piece of cloth, called a *himation,* was often worn wrapped around the body, without a tunic underneath. Young men sometimes wore only a short cloak, called a *chlamys.* For travelling, cloaks were worn over tunics.

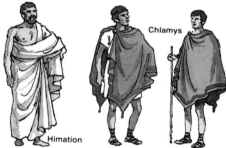

Chlamys

Himation

Hats

Travellers wore caps, or broad-brimmed hats, like these.

Shoes

Many people went barefoot most of the time. Sandals were the most common form of footwear for both men and women, although boots and shoes were worn sometimes.

Jewellery

Archaeologists have found some magnificent Ancient Greek jewellery. The Greeks were especially good at gold and silver work and used enamels to give a touch of colour. Until the Hellenistic Period, coloured gemstones were not widely used except in rings. Cheap jewellery was made from bronze, iron and lead.

Pins and brooches were used to fasten tunics and cloaks. Decorated metal rosettes have been found which may have been sewn on to very expensive clothes.

Rings were made entirely of metal or with a carved, coloured stone. Some were in the form of signet rings.

A lot of Greek women wore drop earrings. Some were very elaborate and detailed.

Various styles of jewelled headbands, or diadems, were worn by noblewomen. Men sometimes wore a plain headband.

Bracelets and armlets were often decorated with animal heads. Another popular design was this snake bracelet.

Women wore many styles of delicately made necklaces and chains. At first men wore very little jewellery – only brooches on their tunics, and rings – but later it became fashionable to wear more.

Make-up and Hairstyles

Make-up and perfume were worn by women who could afford it. They used a powder made from white lead to whiten their faces and rouge to make their cheeks pink. The eyes and lips were painted too. A mixture containing arsenic was used to remove unwanted hair from the body.

Instead of using soap the Greeks rubbed their bodies with oil. When they scraped it off, the dirt came off with it.

This painting shows a girl washing her hair. Fair hair was fashionable for a time and some women dyed their hair or wore wigs.

Mirror

Aryballoi (perfume flasks)

Alabastron (oil jar)

Comb   Pyxides (powder jars)

This mirror and the jars and flasks for cosmetics would have belonged to a wealthy Greek woman.

Hairstyles

Women grew their hair to at least shoulder length and had it arranged in curls. It was worn loose or piled on top in various different styles, and held in place by pins, ribbons and scarves. Here is a selection of styles.

Greek men had short or, at most, shoulder length hair. Most of them wore beards, though the younger ones were often clean shaven. By the Hellenistic Period, beards had started going out of fashion.

The barber's shop was a good place to go and meet friends, while you had your hair and beard trimmed.

79

Shopping and Money

The marketplace in a Greek city was called the *agora*. In Athens it was surrounded by important public buildings. Traders set up stalls in the open air or in the *stoa* (the colonnade). Others sold goods straight from their workshops. It was usually the men who did the shopping. The richer ones would take a slave with them to carry the purchases home. The *agora* was also a place where men went to meet their friends. Employers went to hire workmen or buy slaves.

Restaurant
Potter's shop

In Athens, officials were appointed to check the weights and measures and the quality of goods on sale.

In early times there was no money, so people bartered (exchanged goods that they agreed were of similar value).

Later, goods were exchanged for an agreed amount of metal, such as gold, silver, copper or iron.

The first coins

Coins were being made in Lydia, a Greek colony in Turkey, sometime before 600BC. Electrum (a mixture of gold and silver) was made into pieces of exactly the same weight and purity. They were stamped by the government to certify this. Later, other Greek cities adopted their own coinage.

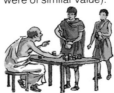

When you visited another city, you had to go to a moneychanger who, for a fee, would change your coins for you.

Later, banks were set up. Bankers lent their own and their clients' money to customers, who had to repay the money with interest.

Coins

Greek coins were made of gold or silver. At first each coin was stamped with the symbol of its city. Later gods and goddesses were shown, and later still, portraits of rulers. The most common Greek coin was the *drachma*. In Athens there were six *obols* to one *drachma*, two *drachmae** to one *stater*, 50 *staters* to one *mina*, and 60 *minae* to one *talent*. Here is a selection of coins from different cities.

Early electrum coin from Lydia, from the reign of King Croesus (c. 561-546BC)

Early gold coin with writing on it. Origin unknown.

Coin from Corinth, showing Pegasus, the winged horse.

Coin from Peparethus. c. 500BC.

Coin from Syracuse, showing the head of the nymph, Arethusa c. 415BC.

Coin from Athens, with an owl, the symbol of Athens. c. 500BC.

Coin from Syracuse, showing Arethusa and some dolphins. c. 479BC.

Coin from Macedon, showing King Philip of Macedon. c. 360-338BC.

*The plural of drachma.   **c. stands for* circa, *which means "about".*

81

Family Life

When a baby was born, the mother presented it to the father. If he refused to accept it, it was put out to die.

Once the baby was accepted, celebrations were held to present it to the gods and give it a name.

In wealthy families the child was put into the care of a nurse, who often looked after it until it grew up.

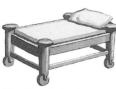

The Greeks had some furniture made specially for babies. This cot on wheels was shown in a painting.

This is a high chair. Some chairs had a potty placed in the lower part of the stand.

This baby's feeding bottle and rattle in the shape of a pig were found on the sites of Ancient Greek houses.

Toys and games

Up to the age of seven, Greek children had nothing to do but play. Here are some of their toys and the games they played.

Ball games

Doll   Toy goose and rider

Rolling hoops

Riding in a cart

Yo-yo

Playing on swings

82

At 18, a boy officially came of age. There were celebrations and garlands of flowers were hung on the doors.

When a girl was about 15, her father chose a husband for her. The groom was often much older, as many Greek men delayed marrying for a long time. Here the bride is being dressed and prepared for the ceremony.

Wedding celebrations began at the bride's home with a sacrifice at the altar. The bride was crowned and presented to the groom by her father. Then she was led to her new home in a procession led by musicians and a torch bearer.

The groom carried the bride over the threshold. Then they made an offering to the gods and shared a special cake together.

Women's lives

Greek women were always under the control of their nearest male relative – their father, husband or son. Husbands were paid a dowry – a gift of money or property – by their father-in-law. This had to be returned if there was a divorce. Men could divorce their wives by sending them away, but women had to act through an official.

Women from wealthy families spent most of their time at home, in the women's quarters. They had to make sure the store rooms were well stocked and the house was clean. They supervised the slave women preparing wool, spinning and weaving.

There was very little opportunity to get out of the house. A rich woman who wanted to do some shopping had to be escorted by a slave.

This did not apply to ordinary women, who had no slaves. They had more freedom as they had to do many things for themselves.

Education

Boys went to school between the ages of seven and 15. All citizens were expected to send their sons to school, but as fees were charged, poor boys probably did not stay very long. A boy from a wealthy family was taken to school by a slave called a *pedagogue,* who would stay during the lessons, possibly helping to keep order in the classroom. Schools taught reading, writing and sums, music, poetry, sport and gymnastics.

Girls were taught at home by their mothers. They learnt the skills needed to run a home, such as cooking, spinning and weaving.

Schoolchildren wrote with a stylus on a wooden tablet covered with wax. You could rub out the mistakes and re-use the tablet.

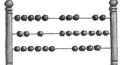

Sums were worked out on a frame called an abacus. The beads were worth one each on the top row, 10 each on the second row and 100 each on the third.

Children read the works of great authors and poets, such as Homer and learnt poetry by heart.

In music lessons they were taught to sing and dance and to play the lyre and the pipes.

Athletics played an important part in a boy's education, especially after the age of 14.

At 18 a boy was a full citizen. He then became an *ephebe,* which meant doing two years military service.

Although there were no universities, men like the philosopher Plato set up schools of further education.

Teachers called sophists taught young men how to present arguments.

Education in Sparta

In Sparta all children belonged to the state. A committee of elders decided if a baby was healthy enough to be allowed to live. At seven, boys were taken away from home and sent to a kind of boarding school, called a *pedonome,* where the discipline was very strict.

A Spartan education aimed to make children tough. The boys were given only one tunic a year to wear. They had no sandals and no bedclothes and they had to sleep on the ground.

They were kept hungry, so they had to steal for food. This was supposed to teach them stealth and cunning and to train them to live off enemy land when they became soldiers.

Most of their training was concerned with making them into good soldiers. They spent a lot of time learning how to use weapons and very little on academic work.

The boys were savagely beaten to teach them courage. There were competitions to see who could suffer most without complaining.

They learnt songs about war and love for their country. Dancing lessons were supposed to make them strong and agile.

The Spartans valued the wisdom of old people. Young Spartans were taught to show respect at all times.

Boys were allowed to attend public dinners, which were held once a month, to enable them to learn from the conversation of the men.

Although Spartan girls did not go to school, they were also brought up to be tough. Their education included wrestling and athletics.

Games, Music and Entertainment

Greek men went regularly to the town sports centre – the *gymnasium* – for exercise, such as wrestling, and to meet friends and talk.

They also played energetic ball games. This carving shows a game which looks rather like hockey.

Setting two cocks to fight to the death was regarded as an exciting sport. Sometimes other animals were used.

The Greeks had board games too. The two soldiers in this vase painting are playing a game that may have been something like draughts.

Knucklebones was a game played with four bones, which you tossed in the air. The sides of the bones were numbered and you needed a certain combination of numbers to win.

Music and dancing

Although music played an important part in Greek education, most professional musicians and dancers were slaves or freed slaves. They were trained at special schools. Some became attached to a family and entertained guests at dinner. Others could be hired for parties and special occasions.

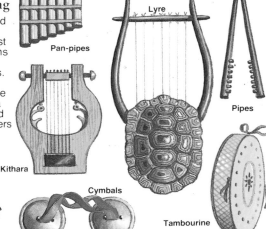

Pan-pipes

Lyre

Kithara

Pipes

Cymbals

Tambourine

Some religious festivals provided an opportunity for ordinary citizens to dance.

Here is a selection of Greek musical instruments. The pan-pipes were named after the god Pan, who was said to have invented them.

Parties

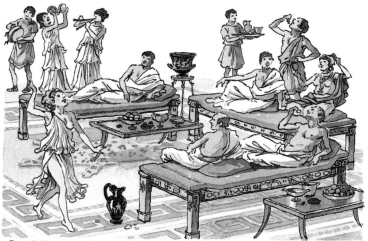

Greek dinner parties were for men only, although some clever and beautiful unmarried women, called *hetairai*, might be invited too. The guests sat around on couches in the *andron* (the dining room), each with his own table. Slaves served the food and presented the guests with wreaths of flowers to wear. After the meal, the men stayed to drink and have a discussion, called a *symposium*.

The Greeks always drank their wine mixed with water. The wine was mixed in a huge jar, called a *krater*.

People ate their food with their fingers. Slaves stood by to wash the guests' fingers between courses.

Cottabos was a popular game played at dinner. You kept some wine in your cup and flicked it at a chosen target.

A whole range of entertainers could be hired for parties. There were jugglers, acrobats, sword dancers, comedians, story tellers and actors as well as dancers accompanied by musicians.

The Olympic Games

The Olympic Games were held once every four years at Olympia, in honour of Zeus, king of the gods. There were other festivals which held sporting events, but these were the most famous. Men came from all over Greece and the colonies to watch them. All wars were postponed for three months to allow people to travel in safety. The Olympic Games probably date back to 776BC.

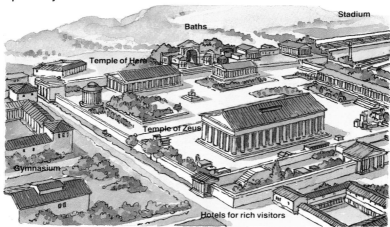

There were temples and altars where people came to worship the gods and make sacrifices. This statue of Zeus, which stood in his temple at Olympia, was 13m high and made of gold and ivory.

The athletes covered their bodies with oil, as a protection against sun and dirt. After the contest, it was scraped off with a curved instrument, called a *strigil*.

Judges watched all the events from a special stand in the stadium. Many of the other spectators had to stand as there were few seats.

The winners were given ribbons, palm branches or wreaths as prizes. They competed for glory, rather than money. At the end of the games there was a huge banquet.

The contests

The Olympic Games lasted for five days. All the athletes were men. One of the contests, the *pentathlon,* was for all-round athletes. This involved taking part in five events – discus, javelin, jumping, running and wrestling – all in one afternoon.

The oldest event was running. The races were either one, two or 24 lengths of the stadium.

In one race the men wore helmets and greaves (leg guards) and carried shields.

Another event was discus-throwing. The discus was a flat, bronze disc, about the size of a dinner plate.

Javelin throwers wound a leather thong round their fingers. This helped them to throw the javelin more smoothly.

Long jumpers carried weights, which they swung forward as they jumped.

Chariot races were included in the games. At one time there were races for chariots drawn by mules.

Horse races and chariot races were held in the *hippodrome**. The jockeys raced without saddles or stirrups.

In wrestling, either the contest went on till one man gave up, or the victor had to throw his opponent three times.

The *pankration* was a violent form of fighting. But there were strict rules and referees kept a look out for fouls.

Boxers wore leather thongs wound round their hands, sometimes with a piece of sheepskin underneath.

There were separate games in which women could take part. These were part of a festival for the goddess Hera.

*Hippo *is the Greek for horse.*

89

The Theatre

Drama developed from the songs and dances performed in Athens at the festival of Dionysus, the god of wine. The songs in the god's honour were sung by a group of 12 to 15 men, called the chorus. Then an actor was included, who talked with the leader of the chorus. As more actors took part, the words and action became more important and proper plays were written.

Skene (stage)

Chorus

Orchestra

Plays were performed in theatres in the open air. Seats for the audience were cut into the slope of a hillside. They were made of wood at first, but were later replaced by stone. The philosopher Plato tells us that in some theatres there was room for up to 30,000 people. Performances lasted all day, with several plays in a row.

These bronze tickets told you which block of seats to sit in. They cost two *obols* each. Poor people could get help from public funds to pay for them.

Important people, such as judges and local officials sat in the front. This seat of honour was for the priest of Dionysus.

Plays were divided into tragedies and comedies. The judges awarded ivy wreaths to the authors of the best tragedy and the best comedy.

Tragedies

Tragedies told sad tales about the conflicts of love, honour and religious duty. They were usually based on stories the audience knew well, such as the Trojan War. This painting shows Queen Clytemnestra killing the Trojan princess, Cassandra.

The chorus sometimes sang and danced, but their main role was making speeches to tell you more about the story.

Comedies

This painting shows a scene from a comedy. Comedies made fun of all kinds of things, including politics, religion and important local personalities.

In comedies the chorus sometimes represented animals. This painting shows them dressed as birds.

Costumes

All the actors wore masks, with different facial expressions. They changed masks to show the changes in mood of the character. Wide mouths in the masks helped them project their voices.

In comedies the actors wore padded clothes to make them look funnier. There were no female actors, so men had to dress as women to play the women's parts.

Scenery

The scenery was usually painted to look like a palace or temple, as shown on this piece of painted pot.

Scene changes were rare. They were probably done by revolving part of the wall, like this.

91

Farming

Many people in Ancient Greece were farmers. Good farming land was scarce though, as much of the country is mountainous and the soil poor. The main crops were wheat, barley, grapes and olives. The best grazing land was in the marshy regions of Thessaly and Boeotia. Elsewhere there was very little good pasture, so only a few farms were able to keep horses or cattle for meat. Most farmers only had oxen for ploughing the fields.

Wheat and barley were grown on the plains. A farmer's year began in October. He ploughed the land, while someone behind him sowed the grain by hand. Every year some of the land was left fallow (not planted), so that the soil could regain its goodness.

The crops grew during the winter when there was rain. In May it was ready to be harvested with sickles.

To thresh the grain, or separate it from the straw, animals were driven over it on paved circular floors. Then it was winnowed (separated from the chaff, or husks). This was done by throwing the grain up into the air, so that the light chaff blew away.

Grapes were grown in vineyards on the lower hill slopes. They were picked in September.

Some grapes were kept for eating and the rest were made into wine. Men trod the grapes with their feet to get the juice out. It was then poured into jars and left to ferment into wine.

To pick olives, men climbed the trees or knocked the olives down with poles. The trees were protected by law and could not be uprooted.

To extract the oil, the olives were crushed in a press, like this. Olive oil was used for cooking, lighting and cleaning the body.

Farmers also grew vegetables. These included peas, beans, turnips, cucumbers, garlic, onions, lettuces, leeks, artichokes, carrots and pumpkins. Fruit and nuts, such as apples, pears, plums, figs, almonds, pomegranates and melons were also grown.

A few wealthy farmers had horses for riding or pulling chariots.

Sheep and goats grazed on the hillsides. Goats supplied meat, milk and cheese. Sheep were kept for wool and some meat.

Farmers also kept pigs and poultry for meat and eggs.

Hunting wild animals, such as deer, hares and wild boars, was a way of supplementing the food produced on farms.

What the Greeks ate

Most people in Ancient Greece lived mainly on a kind of porridge, bread, cheese, fruit, vegetables and eggs. Meat was a rare treat, unless you were rich. Breakfast and lunch were both fairly light meals. The main meal was in the evening.

As most Greeks lived near the sea, fish, eaten fresh or dried, was an important source of protein.

They used honey to sweeten their food, as they had no sugar. Bees were kept in pottery hives.

People's Jobs

Many Greeks earned their living as craftsmen. The skills were probably passed down from father to son, or through another member of the family. Most workshops were small. They were run by a family with their slaves – probably six men in all, though there were some large businesses using a lot of slaves. Some men kept slaves specially for hiring out to employers in need of extra workmen. Greek women worked in the home.

Carpenters made furniture, parts of weapons and tools and were employed in building work. These men are finishing off a chest.

Pottery

The kiln has been cut away, so you can see inside.

Air vent

Pottery was an important craft as potters made many household goods, such as lamps and cooking pots. First they dug clay and mixed it with water. One potter shaped the pot while his assistant turned the wheel. Then the pot was fired (baked) in a kiln.

Painting pots

The Greek art of painting pottery was admired all over the Ancient World. First the design was painted on the unfired pot with a mixture of clay, water and probably wood ash. The pot was put in the kiln to begin the firing process. Then all the openings in the kiln were closed. The lack of air made the pot turn black. Air was then allowed in again. The painted parts stayed black and the rest of the pot turned red. This process might have taken years to get right.

Mining

This man is working in a silver mine. Mines and quarries were owned by the state and leased to private citizens. They employed a lot of slaves, often in very bad conditions.

Iron working

Iron was used mainly for tools and weapons. Iron ore was mixed with charcoal and put into a furnace. Lumps of metal formed at the bottom, which were reheated before being hammered into shape.

Bronze working

The Greeks were experts at the "lost wax" method of bronze working. First a clay core was made and pins stuck in it. The statue was modelled round the core in wax and then the whole thing was covered with clay. The clay-covered model was heated, which made the wax melt and run out. The core was still held in place by the pins.

Molten bronze was poured in where the wax had been. When the bronze had set, the clay mould was removed.

There were other methods of working bronze. It could be poured straight into ordinary moulds (right) or heated a little, to make it soften, and then hammered into shape (left).

Sculpture

Here is a sculptor at work carving a *herm*, a statue of a god which people stood at their front doors. Sculptors made statues of stone, bronze, wood, ivory and gold.

Finishing off a stone statue involved painting it. Greek statues were always painted, either all over or in parts. The paint has since worn away, leaving the bare stone.

Here is a cobbler at work. Some skilled slaves were set up in business by their masters, in return for a share of the profits.

Skilled boat-builders were always in demand to supply boats for fishing, for the navy and for travelling.

Some men worked as part-time fishermen, in order to provide their families with extra food.

Pottery

Greek pots and vases were painted by skilled artists, but they were also strong and practical. They were not treated as ornaments, but were made only for daily use. Here is a guide to help you recognize the main shapes and styles.

Recognizing styles

Pots with **geometric** patterns, like this, date from 900–700BC.

The **protogeometric** style dates from 1000 to 900BC. Look out for circles or semi-circles on the design.

The 6th century BC was the period of the **orientalizing style,** ▶ influenced by the East. The decoration includes animals and plants.

Black figure ware – black figures on a reddish background – was produced between 600 and 530BC.

Red figure ware – red figures on a black background – dates from 530BC.

Figures painted on a white background are found on vases dating from 500BC.

Some potters made cups in the form of animal or human heads.

From about 400BC, the standard of pottery declined. Pots either imitated metal vases (above), or were fussy and over-decorated.

Recognizing shapes

Amphorae were used for storing wine. They are one of the most common types of pot.

A *stamnos* (left) and a *pelike* (right) were also storage jars.

 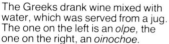

The Greeks drank wine mixed with water, which was served from a jug. The one on the left is an *olpe,* the one on the right, an *oinochoe.*

Some cups were large, so that they could be passed round all the guests at a ceremony. The handles were designed so that people lying on couches could hold them easily.

Greek women carried water in a jar, called a *hydria.* It was specially designed with three handles.

Kraters were bowls for mixing wine and water. The one on the left is called a *volute krater.*

A *kyathos* was a ladle. It was used for serving wine from a *krater* into cups and jugs.

Oils and perfumes were kept in small bottles, like these – an *aryballos* (left), an *alabastron* (centre) and a *lekythos* (right). The pot on the far right is a *pyxis,* used for storing cosmetics.

Gods and Goddesses

The Greeks believed in many gods and had hundreds of stories about them. There were local gods and gods to look after all aspects of life and death. According to legend, Mother Earth gave birth to all living things. The first gods were called the Titans. Zeus, the son of two Titans called Chronos and Rhea, seized power for himself and his brothers and sisters. In Classical times they were the most important gods. They were called Olympians, as they were said to live on Mount Olympus.

Zeus, god of the sky and thunder, ruled the gods on Mount Olympus. **Hera,** his wife and sister, was goddess of all women.

Demeter, a sister of Zeus, was goddess of the earth and corn.

Aphrodite was goddess of love and beauty. Her son, **Eros,** made people fall in love by shooting them with arrows. **Hephaestos,** her husband, was the gods' craftsman.

Ares was god of war. He loved Aphrodite.

Athene, daughter of Zeus, was goddess of wisdom and Athens. Her symbol was an owl.

Apollo was god of the sun and patron of music, poetry and healing.

Artemis was goddess of the moon, hunting and women.

Poseidon, brother of Zeus, was god of the sea.

Hermes was messenger of the gods and patron of merchants and travellers. He took the dead to the Underworld.

Pluto, Zeus's brother, ruled the Underworld, the world of the dead. Demeter's daughter, **Persephone,** whom he had kidnapped, ruled with him. Demeter's grief over this caused winter, but every year Persephone returned to her mother and so brought the spring. ▶

Dionysus was god of wine.

Lesser gods and spirits

Beneath the great gods and goddesses was a host of divine beings. Here are some of them.

Pan, god of the countryside, was half-goat. He played the pan-pipes.

Asclepius, son of Apollo, was god of medicine. His symbol was snakes.

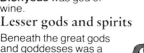

Centaurs were half-men, half-horses.

Nine **muses** looked after music and learning.

Nymphs were beautiful girls who lived in trees and streams.

The **Furies,** were dog-headed, bat-winged creatures, with snakes for hair. They pursued murderers and drove them mad.

Boreas was the north wind.

Charon ferried the dead across the River Styx to the Underworld. **Cerberus** was a three-headed god, who guarded the entrance.

99

Heroes

Many Greek poems and plays are based on the stories of their legendary heroes. Some of them had probably been real people in Mycenaean times, or earlier. As time passed, the stories were changed and added to, until they became full of supernatural deeds. Here are a few of the main characters.

Herakles was given 12 impossible tasks, which included fighting terrible monsters. He succeeded and became a god.

Theseus killed the Minotaur, a monster which lived in Crete, in an underground maze, or labyrinth, and ate humans.

There were many stories about the Trojan War. This was caused by the elopement of Paris, a prince of Troy, with Queen Helen of Sparta.

The Greeks went to Troy to try to get her back. After a ten year siege, the Trojans were defeated. The Greeks tricked them by hiding soldiers inside a wooden horse, which they presented to the Trojans as a gift.

The Odyssey tells of the hero, Odysseus, and of the many things that happened to him on his way back from the Trojan War.

Jason and his companions, the Argonauts, sailed in search of the Golden Fleece. They won it with the help of Princess Medea.

Jason married Medea, but then deserted her. In revenge, she killed their children and escaped in a chariot drawn by dragons.

Oedipus, ignorant of his real identity, killed his father and married his mother. This enraged the gods and brought disaster.

Perseus wore winged sandals that enabled him to fly. He killed the Gorgon Medusa and rescued a princess from a sea monster.

Bellerophon tamed the winged horse, Pegasus, and so was able to kill the lion-headed, serpent-tailed, fire-breathing Chimera.

Religion

Greek houses had altars for family worship. People burnt incense there, made offerings of food and said prayers to the god or goddess they felt could help them best.

A temple was the home of a god or goddess. This is a model of an early temple, which would have been made of brick or wood. It had a chamber, called a *cella* and a columned porch.

As time passed, larger, more elaborate temples were built of stone, with tiled or stone roofs. This is the temple of the Parthenon in Athens, dedicated to the worship of the goddess, Athene.

A statue of the god or goddess stood in the *cella*. Inside the Parthenon was a 12m high statue of Athene, made of gold and ivory. People visited the temple to pray privately, but there were no services inside for a congregation.

The temple treasury contained offerings, such as jewellery, given by people who wanted to win favour with the gods or thank them.

Priests and priestesses were appointed to perform daily rituals in the service of the god or goddess, such as burning incense or presenting food offerings. A few temples had special priestesses who were young girls.

Festivals

The Greeks had many festivals to celebrate the feast days of their gods and goddesses. An animal was sacrificed at a special altar outside the temple. The sex, colour and type of animal was different for each god. There were hymns and prayers, and incense was burned. When praying to an Underworld god, you held the palms of your hands downwards. For the other gods, the palms faced upwards. There were usually processions and often theatrical and athletic competitions too.

The most important festival in Athens was the Great Panathenia, the feast of the goddess Athene. A procession led to the Parthenon, taking a beautiful new robe to Athene. It was held every four years, with a less splendid festival on the years in between.

People often sang and danced in the processions. The festivals in honour of Dionysus often became very wild. The worshippers were drunk with wine, and were known to kill animals, and even people, until efforts were made to control them.

In the Anthesteria festival of Dionysus at Athens, three year old children took part and were given tiny jugs, like these, as presents.

Mystery cults

A mystery cult was a secret cult associated with a particular god or goddess. The most famous was that of Demeter and Persephone at Eleusis. You joined in stages and learned a new secret at each stage. The members never revealed the secrets, so we know very little about them.

This scene shows what may have happened at the final initiation ceremony at Eleusis. The new member is received into the cult by the goddesses themselves, who were priestesses acting the parts.

Messages from the gods

The Greeks believed that priests called soothsayers could interpret messages from the gods. They thought that things such as thunderstorms, dreams and the birth of a deformed animal were messages from the gods.

By watching the flight of birds or examining the insides of a sacrificed animal, they could find out if the gods favoured something.

Oracles

If you wanted a direct answer from a god to a difficult problem, you could ask an oracle. The most famous was the oracle of Apollo at Delphi. You sent the god a written question. Then a priestess, called the Pythia, went into a trance and spoke for the god. A priest interpreted her often confused replies.

Funerals and the Underworld

A dead person was dressed in white and laid in state in the house, so friends and relatives could pay their last respects.

The next day the body was taken to the tomb – in a carriage if the family were wealthy. A procession followed with music and professional women mourners. The body, or its burnt ashes, was then placed in the tomb, with offerings of food and personal possessions.

People went on making regular offerings to their dead relatives long after the funeral.

The Greeks believed dead people went to the Underworld, a grey, shadowy kingdom where ordinary people just roamed around. The wicked were given punishments, but the very good were granted eternal happiness in the Elysian Fields.

Greek Armies

In the Classical Period each city state had its own army. All citizens were expected to fight whenever they were needed. There was almost always a war going on somewhere in Greece. When one city wanted to fight another, an animal was sacrificed and its insides were examined, to see if the gods were in favour of a war. Then a herald was sent to declare war. The Athenian army was commanded by ten generals.

Spear · Corinthian helmet · Breastplate · Protective apron · Shield · Thracian helmet · Sword · Chalcidian helmet · Greaves (leg guards)

Here is a selection of the armour and weapons that were used. Each soldier had to provide his own. Poor citizens, who could not afford to buy armour, usually joined the navy and became rowers instead.

Greek men were taught how to fight when they were at school. In battle, they fought shoulder to shoulder in a formation called a phalanx. They usually threw their spears and then charged at the enemy to try to break their ranks.

Thessaly and Boeotia had cavalry, but most armies used mounted soldiers only as scouts.

The Spartan army

Spartan soldiers were the most feared of all the Greeks. Their education system was specially designed to produce good, obedient soldiers. Even after they married, at the age of 30, they continued to live in the military barracks. The Spartan army was commanded by one of the two Spartan kings*.

Each army usually had a small force of archers and another of lightly armed javelin throwers.

This vase painting shows a wounded soldier being bandaged.

In the Hellenistic Period, cavalry played a more important role. Philip of Macedon and his son, Alexander, were both brilliant commanders, who used infantry and cavalry together.

They favoured lighter armour, so that the soldiers could move more quickly. Much longer pikes were used, up to 6m in length.

Siege warfare

A tactic often used was to destroy the enemy's crops. The army then tried to surround the city by land and sea, to cut off new supplies.

The historian, Thucydides, described a flame-thrower used in a seige. Huge bellows blasted air down a tube into a cauldron of burning tar. Flames from the cauldron were blown forward and spread all around.

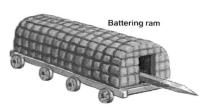

Catapult

Siege tower

Battering ram

By about 400BC, the Greeks had started using battering rams to attack enemy walls and catapults which fired javelins. Siege towers were used to enable soldiers to climb on to enemy walls.

Sea battles

Battles were often fought at sea. Tactics included ramming enemy ships and manoeuvring to break their oars. Once close to an enemy ship, the soldiers would try to board it and fight.

Travel

At night, people took flaming torches with them, as there was no street lighting.

Most people in Greece went everywhere on foot. On longer journeys they might take a walking stick and a folding stool, so that they could rest along the way. The wealthy travelled on horseback or in horse-drawn chariots.

Bandits and the frequent wars between states made travelling in some parts of the country very dangerous.

Only a few busy routes had reasonable roads and there were hardly any bridges. In winter, carts and chariots often got stuck in the mud. For transporting goods it was easier to use donkeys or mules.

Although there were some wayside inns, they did not always offer food. People considered it a duty to offer hospitality to any traveller in need of shelter.

Sea travel

Where possible long journeys were made by sea, instead of overland. The best time for sailing was in the summer. Sea travel had its dangers too – from storms, rocky coasts and pirates. Many wrecks have been found by underwater archaeologists.

The Navy

Of all the city states, Athens had the most powerful navy. It was financed by a rich vein of silver discovered in their silver mines at Laureum in 483BC. With their fleet they were able to win many vital sea battles against their great enemies, the Persians, and to prevent an attempted invasion. Positions such as captain or helmsman were held by trained sailors, but ordinary men were employed as rowers.

Among the earliest warships were the *penteconters*. These were long ships with 50 oarsmen.

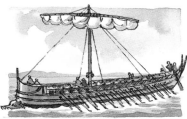

Later, the Greeks started using two banks of oarsmen on each side of the ship to give it greater speed and

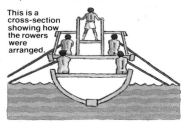

This is a cross-section showing how the rowers were arranged.

make it easier to manoeuvre. This kind of ship was called a *bireme*.

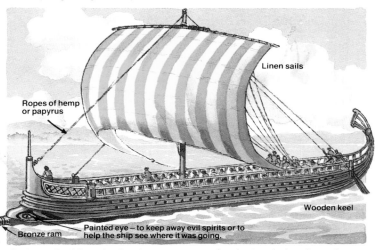

Linen sails

Ropes of hemp or papyrus

Wooden keel

Bronze ram

Painted eye – to keep away evil spirits or to help the ship see where it was going.

A *trireme* had three banks of oars, and 170 rowers, though experts differ as to how it was arranged. There was an upper deck for the soldiers to fight on. Ships went to sea for short periods only, as there was little space for cooking and sleeping. Later, *quadriremes* and *quinqueremes,* with four and five banks of oars, were built.

Trade and the Colonies

The Greek city states sold their surplus goods by trading with each other and with other lands around the Mediterranean and Black Seas. There were no large trading companies. Each merchant usually had his own ship. Some traders were rich enough to finance their own deals, but many had to borrow from bankers. In Athens, many of the richest traders were *metics* (foreigners). They were forbidden by law to own land, so many invested in trade instead.

The goods were usually sent in sturdy sailing ships, like these. To navigate, they used the stars and well-known landmarks.

Goods to be delivered inland were sent across country on the backs of mules.

Here are two traders from different parts of Greece negotiating a deal. Payment was in coins.

The main exports from Greece were wine, olive oil and manufactured goods, such as cloth, pots and statues.

Imports included grain from the Black Sea, copper, tin, timber and goods from Africa and the East, such as ivory, incense, spices, perfume, silk and slaves.

The Greeks travelled far in search of trade. This scene, based on a vase painting, shows a trader supervising the loading of a cargo at Cyrene in North Africa.

Explorers

In 300 BC, Pytheas of Massilia (Marseilles) explored northern Europe. He claimed to have sailed round the British Isles, but few believed his account of his trip.

In 120 BC, a trader called Eudoxus met a shipwrecked Indian sailor who showed him how to use the monsoon winds. This enabled him to sail to India and back.

The colonies

At the time of the Dorian invasions, many people left Greece and set up colonies in Ionia, on the west coast of what is now Turkey. The next wave of colonization began in the 8th century BC. A rise in population had led to a serious shortage of farming land and many left to seek their fortunes abroad.

Families of emigrants set off with animals and supplies of food and seed for planting. They settled in largely uninhabited areas and built new cities, modelled on the Greek ones.

A map of Greek settlements

This map shows the extent of Greek settlements. The new cities provided raw materials and markets for Greek goods. They were completely independent, though fellow Greeks sometimes came to their aid when they were threatened by enemies. A tribe called the Graii settled in Italy. The Romans later called them Graeci. This word came to be used for all who spoke their language, and from it comes our word "Greek".

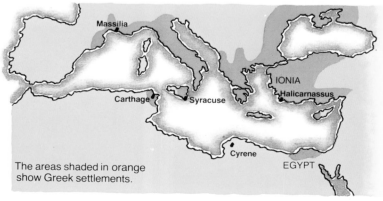

The areas shaded in orange show Greek settlements.

The Government

How city states grew up

Rulers in Mycenaean times often built their palaces in high places which could be defended easily. People settled inside the walls.

These settlements grew into towns and then cities, spreading beyond the original walls. New walls were built to enclose them.

By Classical times, Greece was divided into many small city states, each consisting of a city and the countryside and villages around it.

Types of government

In Mycenaean times, the states of Greece were ruled by kings, assisted by their nobles.

By about 800BC, most kings were replaced by oligarchies, small groups of aristocrats (from *aristoi,* meaning best people).

Many people felt their needs were ignored by the oligarchs, so they helped tyrants* to gain power. Some tyrants were good rulers, but others were cruel and unjust.

By the beginning of the Classical Period, tyrants were being replaced by democracies. In a democracy, all citizens have a say in the government. In Ancient Greece, only men could be citizens. The states were small, so most men were able to attend meetings and were encouraged to take an active part in politics. The word politics comes from the Greek word *polis,* meaning city.

In Athens, an assembly was held three or four times a month. All citizens could attend, speak and vote on government policies.

Policies to be submitted to the assembly were decided on by the council, a group of 500 men. For political purposes, the citizens of Athens were divided into ten tribes. The council contained 50 men from each tribe. Each tribe took it in turn to lead the council. Councillors served for a year.

Tyrants were men who ruled single-handed.

At first nine men called *archons* were the chief officials. Later, they were replaced in importance by ten generals, called *strategoi,* who were elected each year by the assembly.

There was a host of lesser officials to see to the day to day running of government. They were chosen by lot, which meant that even poor citizens had the chance of becoming officials.

Poor citizens were paid a day's wage to attend the assembly. This was to enable them to take an active part in government.

Wealthy citizens were expected to make extra contributions to the state, such as paying for warships, or a new play at the theatre.

This is Perikles, a popular politician who was re-elected in Athens every year between 460 and 430BC.

To keep check on officials, there was a system called ostracism. Citizens wrote the names of officials they disapproved of on *ostraca,* pieces of broken pottery.

If a certain number of people voted against an official in this way, he was banished from Athens for ten years.

Non-citizens

There were several categories of Athenians who were not citizens. These were women, *metics* (foreigners living permanently in Athens), slaves and freed slaves. If a citizen married a foreigner, his sons could not become citizens.

Household slaves could buy their freedom by saving tips they had earned. Some were granted freedom as part of their master's will.

Slaves who were hired out for work by their masters were paid one-sixth of the wages they earned.

111

Law

In Athens most law cases were tried by juries of over 200 men who were chosen by lot. People volunteered to be jurors. Their names were written on tickets and put into the slots of an "allotment" machine (right). Coloured balls were dropped into the machine, to determine which names would be chosen.

Poor citizens who came forward as jurors were given a day's pay, to enable them to take their turn in court.

There were no lawyers, so citizens had to conduct their own cases in court. Some sought the help of professional speech-writers.

Foreigners were not allowed to speak in court, so they had to get a citizen to act for them.

To avoid long speeches, a water clock was used to limit the time allowed to each speaker. The jar was filled with water to just below the rim and the water dripped out through a hole in the bottom.

The jurors gave their verdicts on the case with ballot discs. The discs with solid knobs meant "innocent", the ones with hollow knobs meant "guilty".

A different system was used for trials involving murder or treason. Treason trials were heard and judged by the whole assembly. Cases of murder were judged by officials in a special court.

The Athenian Law against Tyranny of 336BC is recorded on this tablet. It states that there is no punishment for murdering a tyrant (someone who tries to overthrow democracy and seize power for himself).

Government and Society in Sparta

In about 600BC, the Spartan ruling classes began to cut themselves off from other states and dedicated themselves to war against rival states and rebellious subjects. Spartan citizens (who were all men) became full-time soldiers, living permanently in barracks.

At the age of 30, they were divided by election into "equals" and "inferiors". Only equals had full political rights and could attend the assembly. At the assembly, people voted for or against proposals by shouting.

The proposals to be put to the assembly were decided by a council of elders, a group of men over 60, who were elected by the assembly.

Above the council were five officials, called *ephors,* who were elected each year to run the government.

They were also two Spartan kings, who acted as both military and religious leaders.

The Spartan territory was made up of the provinces of Laconia and Messenia. They had one valuable natural resource – iron.

All the jobs in trade and industry were done by Spartan subjects, called *periokoi.* They were not citizens, but were allowed some say in local affairs and could serve in the army. This left the citizens free to devote themselves to war.

All farming work was done by the helots, descendants of the people who had lived in Sparta before the invasion of the Dorians*. The helots were little more than slaves, producing food for the Spartans.

Many helots were discontented and tried to rebel against their rulers, but the rebellions were always crushed.

*The Spartan rulers were descendants of the Dorians.

113

Architecture

Architectural styles in many parts of the world have been based on those of the Ancient Greeks. The Greeks used their knowledge of mathematics to produce buildings with beautiful proportions. At first the materials used were sun-dried bricks and wood, but these were replaced by limestone and, later, marble.

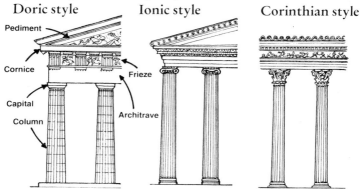

Doric style

Pediment

Cornice

Frieze

Capital

Architrave

Column

Ionic style

Corinthian style

Greek architecture is divided into two main styles – the Doric and the Ionic. A later style, the Corinthian, developed from the Ionic. You can recognize these styles from the types of columns used. This picture shows the names of the different parts of the front of a temple.

Sometimes a *caryatid,* a figure of a girl, took the place of an ordinary column. ► The most famous are in the Erechtheion in Athens.

A circular building was called a *tholos.* Most were used as religious shrines, but there was one in Athens which was used for council meetings.

This eight-sided building is the Tower of the Winds in Athens, which is still intact. It was built to house a huge water clock.

A colonnade like this was called a *stoa.* These were built round markets and other places, to protect people from the sun and rain.

Monuments

Monuments of various kinds were built to honour people and great events.

These are monuments marking graves.

The lion of Chaeronea marks the site of an important battle won by King Philip of Macedon.

Lysicrates built this to commemorate a prize he had won in the theatre.

The great altar at Pergamon was erected in the first century BC. The carvings on it tell the tale of a war between gods and giants.

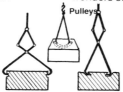

The tomb of King Mausolus (from whom we get the word mausoleum) was so magnificent that it once counted as one of the seven wonders of the world.

Building methods

Public buildings were made from blocks of stone cut from quarries. Teams of workmen hauled the blocks into place. From Greek authors we know that pulleys were also used to lift blocks, but no picture or actual pulley has survived.

Pulleys

Grooves cut into blocks of stone give us an idea of how they were gripped by the pulleys.

Instead of using cement, the Greeks joined blocks of stone together with bronze or iron cramps, like these.

Columns were held together with wooden pegs placed in the top and bottom of each section.

Town planning ▶

By the Classical Period, new Greek cities were being planned on a grid system. The streets were laid out in rows which crossed at right angles.

115

Sculpture and Craftwork

Greek sculptors made statues and carvings for temples, tombs and monuments. The most common subjects were gods, goddesses and heroes. Statues were made from a variety of materials, including marble, limestone, bronze, wood, terracotta, ivory and gold. Most of the surviving statues were made of stone. Many bronze statues were melted down and the metal reused.

Archaic Period

Statues from the Archaic Period look stiff and formal. They were based on Egyptian and eastern styles. The statues are of three main types: the seated figure, the *kouros* (standing youth) and the *kore* (standing girl).

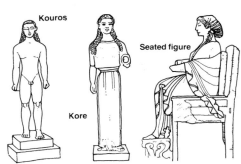

Kouros

Seated figure

Kore

Classical Period

By Classical times, the Greeks had learned how to portray the human body in a completely life-like way. Skilled portraits of important people began to be made as well as sculptures showing scenes and actions. Faces in the scenes often showed expression and emotion, although the ones in portraits were always calm and composed.

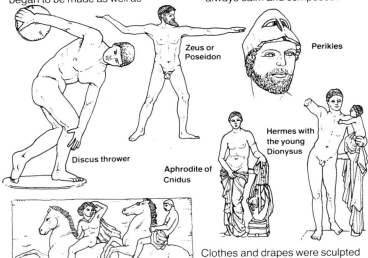

Zeus or Poseidon

Perikles

Discus thrower

Aphrodite of Cnidus

Hermes with the young Dionysus

Clothes and drapes were sculpted with graceful, natural folds. Here are two statues (one a Roman copy, the other probably an original) by the famous Greek sculptor, Praxiteles.

Hellenistic Period

By the Hellenistic Period, a much wider range of subjects was chosen. Outstanding portraits were produced and children, foreigners, old age and suffering were depicted in a realistic way.

Terracottas

Terracottas are small statues made of baked clay. The early ones were made individually, but later some were made in moulds. Terracottas were brightly painted and were usually made as offerings to the gods or the dead. Here is a selection, ranging from the early, rather stiff looking figures, to the later ones, some of which show everyday scenes.

Metalwork

Gold, silver, bronze and iron were used to make a wide range of tableware, jewellery, weapons and other objects. Goods made by Greek craftsmen were in great demand abroad, and have been found by archaeologists all over Europe, South Russia and in the Near and Middle East.

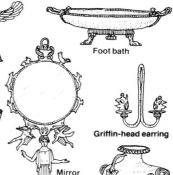

Statuette

Foot bath

Bowl

Griffin-head earring

Mirror

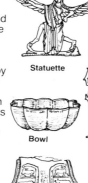

Diadem

Breast plate

Hydria

Learning and Inventions

Greek scholars looked into all aspects of the world around them. The Greeks called these scholars philosophers, although they studied subjects which we would divide into different categories, such as mathematics, astronomy, geology, or medicine. Some of their ideas were based on those of older civilizations, but they also made new and original discoveries, some of which provide the foundations for what we learn today.

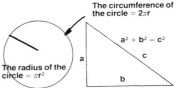

The circumference of the circle = $2\pi r$

The radius of the circle = πr^2

$a^2 + b^2 = c^2$

The greatest mathematicians were Pythagoras, Euclid and Archimedes. They worked out rules in geometry, such as Pythagoras's theorem on triangles and the *"pi"* theorem.

The Greeks studied the stars. This led one scholar to realize that the Earth floated freely in space. Older theories had suggested that it needed something to hold it up.

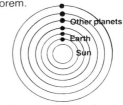

Other planets
Earth
Sun

The astronomer Aristarchus deduced that the Earth turned on its axis, while it and the other planets revolved round the sun.

A later Greek scholar, Ptolemy, believed that the Earth was the centre of the universe, as shown in this diagram. His theory was accepted until the 16th century.

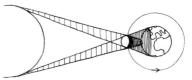

Another Greek put forward the correct explanation for eclipses, and the great scholar Thales was said to have predicted the solar eclipse of 585BC.

Alexandria

Syene

Eratosthenes worked out the distance round the Earth to within 200 miles. He did this by measuring the angle of the sun at Alexandria, and the distance from Alexandria to Syene, where the sun was overhead at noon.

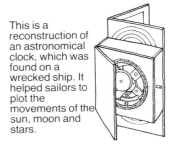

This is a reconstruction of an astronomical clock, which was found on a wrecked ship. It helped sailors to plot the movements of the sun, moon and stars.

Alexandrian inventions

Scientific progress was made by Greeks in Alexandria. This 120m tall lighthouse was designed and built there by architects using advanced engineering techniques. There were bronze mirrors at the top to reflect the light.

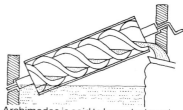

Archimedes is said to have designed this screw, a device for lifting water from one level to another. This method is still used today.

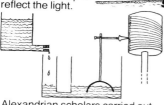

Alexandrian scholars carried out experiments to power machines by water and steam, but they were never put into use. This diagram shows a design for a water-driven clock.

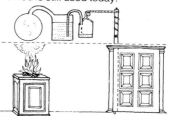

This complicated device was intended to make temple doors open when a fire was lit on the altar.

New tools and techniques

By the 2nd century BC, a new kind of anchor had been developed, that would hold firm even in very rough seas.

An improvement in the design of the potter's wheel allowed the potter to turn the wheel with his foot.

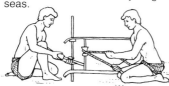

The lathe was probably invented by a Greek. A piece of wood was rotated on a spindle by a man pulling a string, while another man cut the wood with a chisel.

Iron-working was made easier by the introduction of welding. This involved joining pieces of iron by heating them, and then hammering them together on an anvil.

119

Medicine

 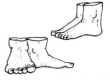

In early times, people tried to cure their illnesses with home-made remedies. If these failed, they might visit the temple of Asclepius, the god of medicine. By sleeping in the temple, the god or his snakes might appear in a dream to cure them. The priests also acted as doctors.

People who were cured sometimes made an offering in the form of a model of the cured part of the body.

Hippocrates

The founder of modern medicine is said to be Hippocrates of Cos, who lived in the 5th century BC. He and his followers saw that diseases had natural causes and were not sent by the gods as punishments. They stressed the importance of finding out all about the patient and his symptoms, in order to provide the correct diagnosis and treatment.

By the 5th century BC, Greek doctors were finding out how the human body worked, by cutting up and examining dead bodies.

Greek doctors prescribed herbal medicines, as well as rest and exercise. This drawing is from a manuscript giving recipes for medicines made from plants.

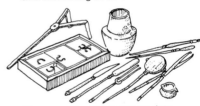

These surgical instruments date from the Hellenistic Period. Without modern drugs to kill pain and germs, operations were painful and dangerous. They were avoided whenever possible.

Studying fossils

Scholars studied the fossils of sea creatures found on land and deduced that the land had once been covered by sea. They concluded that all creatures, including humans, were descended from fish-like creatures.

Rich people paid to have the doctor of their choice. There were also some doctors paid for by the state, so that the poor could be treated free of charge.

Writers and Writing

The alphabet

Greek letter		Name of letter	English equivalent
A	α	alpha	a
B	β	beta	b
Γ	γ	gamma	g
Δ	δ	delta	d
E	ε	epsilon	e
Z	ζ	zeta	z
H	η	eta	e
Θ	θ	theta	th
I	ι	iota	i
K	κ	kappa	k
Λ	λ	lambda	l
M	μ	mu	m
N	ν	nu	n
Ξ	ξ	xi	x (ks)
O	o	omicron	o
Π	π	pi	p
P	ρ	rho	r
Σ	σ	sigma	s
T	τ	tau	t
Y	υ	ypsilon	ü, y
Φ	φ	phi	ph
X	χ	chi	kh, ch
Ψ	ψ	psi	ps
Ω	ω	omega	o

Poetry

The poet Homer lived in the 9th century BC. He told the story of the Trojan Wars in his poems, the *Iliad* and the *Odyssey*. This kind of poetry is called epic poetry.

History

Herodotus is called "The Father of History", as he was the first writer to try to distinguish between fact and legend. In his nine books, the *Historiai**, he wrote about the Persian Wars and his own travels.

Chart of Greek writers and philosophers

Socrates	469-399BC	Philospher. He encouraged people to question all their beliefs.
Plato	428-348BC	Philosopher. He founded a famous school called the Academy. His writings include *Dialogues* and *The Republic*.
Aristotle	384-322BC	Philosopher. He was Plato's pupil and taught Alexander the Great for a time. His writings include *Politics*.
Aeschylus	525-456BC	Writer of Tragedies. The most famous is *The Oresteia*.
Sophocles	496-407BC	Writer of tragedies. His plays include *Antigone, Electra* and *Oedipus Rex*.
Euripides	485-406BC	Writer of tragedies.
Aristophanes	450-385BC	Writer of Comedies. His plays include *The Birds, The Frogs* and *The Wasps*.
Hesiod	8th century BC	Writer. Wrote a history of the gods and farming.
Thucydides	471-400BC	Historian. He wrote about the war between Athens and Sparta.

*Historiai means "enquiries".

Map of Ancient Greece

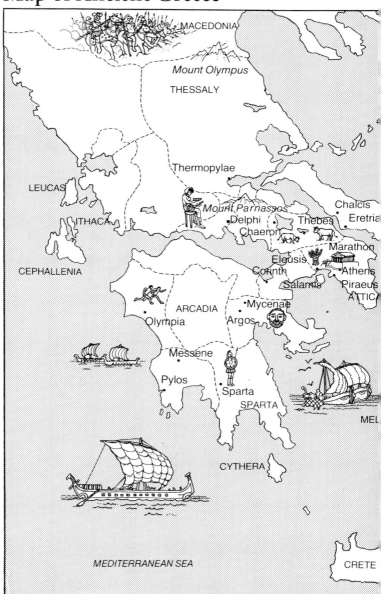

MACEDONIA

Mount Olympus

THESSALY

Thermopylae

LEUCAS

Mount Parnassos

ITHACA

Chalcis

Eretria

Delphi · Thebes ·

Chaeron

CEPHALLENIA

Marathon

Eleusis

Corinth · Athens

Salamis · Piraeus

ATTICA

ARCADIA · Mycenae

· Olympia · Argos

· Messene

MEL

Pylos

· Sparta

SPARTA

CYTHERA

MEDITERRANEAN SEA

CRETE

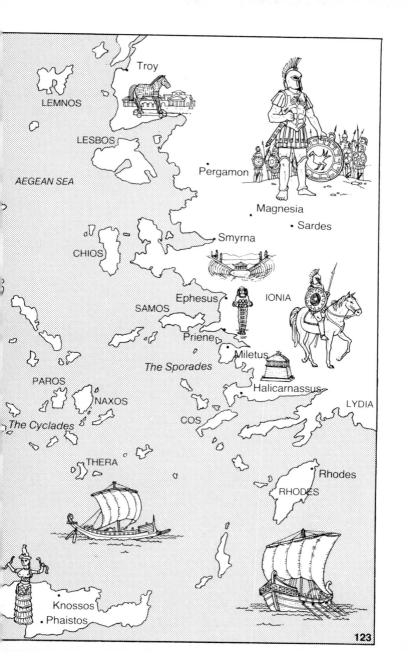

Troy

LEMNOS

LESBOS

AEGEAN SEA

Pergamon

Magnesia

Sardes

Smyrna

CHIOS

Ephesus

IONIA

SAMOS

Priene

The Sporades

Miletus

PAROS

NAXOS

Halicarnassus

LYDIA

The Cyclades

COS

THERA

Rhodes

RHODES

Knossos

Phaistos

The History of Ancient Greece

The earliest inhabitants of Greece were Stone Age hunters. Farming began in about 6000BC. Archaeologists divide the earliest civilizations into Helladic (mainland Greece), Cycladic (the Aegean Islands) and Minoan (Crete).

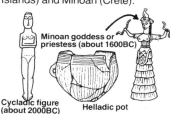

Minoan goddess or priestess (about 1600BC)

Cycladic figure (about 2000BC)

Helladic pot

Between 2200 and 1900BC, people who appear to have spoken an early form of Greek started arriving in Greece. A great civilization grew up, which we name after the city of Mycenae, and which lasted from about 1600 to 1100BC. The Trojan War took place towards the end of this period.

The Dark Ages

Gold mask (about 1500BC)

The period known as the Dark Ages began in about 1100BC. Greece was beset by troubles. The Mycenaeans lost control and a people, called the Dorians, invaded from the north.

During this period, the poet Homer composed *The Iliad* and *The Odyssey*. In the 8th century BC, the Greeks adopted a new, simple alphabet. The population increased and some people emigrated and set up colonies around the Mediterranean.

The Archaic Period

The Archaic Period was a time of political change. Kings had been replaced in power by nobles, who set up oligarchies. In many states, the oligarchies were then overthrown by tyrants, supported by the people. In 594BC, Solon, the ruler of Athens, granted a constitution which marked the first step towards democracy.

The Classical Period

The Classical Period is the time when Athens was at the height of its power. In 499BC, Greek cities in Asia Minor rebelled against their Persian rulers. Athens sent help, but the revolt failed and the Persians declared war against Athens.

The first Persian invasion ended in their defeat at Marathon in 490BC. In 480BC, Sparta and its allies fought the Persians at Thermopylae, but were defeated. In the same year, the Athenians won a great naval victory over the Persians at Salamis. The wars came to an end in 479BC, when the Persians were beaten at Plataea.

In Athens, there followed a golden age in the arts and learning. Many of the finest sculptures and painted pots were produced during this period. Athens formed the Delian League with other Greek states and dominated Greece politically.

In 432BC, the building of the Parthenon in Athens was completed.

Between about 460 and 430BC, Athenian politics were influenced by the brilliant and popular politician, Perikles.

The Peloponnesian Wars were fought between Athens and Sparta from 431 to 404BC. Athens was defeated and the Spartans installed their own government, though democracy was soon restored. The philosopher, Socrates, was forced to commit suicide in 399BC by those seeking to blame someone for the misfortunes of Athens.

Peace did not return to Greece. In 371BC, the Thebans defeated the Spartans. Meanwhile, the power of King Philip of Macedon (above) was growing. He fought many battles and eventually united Greece under his rule.

The Hellenistic Period

In 336BC, Philip was assassinated and succeeded by his son, Alexander the Great (336-323BC). Alexander conquered a vast empire, stretching from Egypt to India. In 331BC, the city of Alexandria was founded in Egypt and it became a centre of learning. After Alexander's death, his generals fought each other and divided the empire between them.

By this time, the Romans were beginning to acquire their own empire. First they took over the Greek colonies in Italy, then moved into Greece itself. Many Greeks were taken to Italy as slaves, and by 146BC, Greece had become a Roman province.

Museums and Sites

Here are the names of some museums where you can find interesting collections of Ancient Greek objects.

Australia

National Gallery of Victoria, **Melbourne,** Victoria.
Nicholson Museum of Antiquities, University of Sydney, **Sydney,** New South Wales.

Canada

Royal Ontario Museum, University of Toronto, **Toronto,** Ontario.

United Kingdom

Birmingham City Museum and Art Gallery, **Birmingham.**
Fitzwilliam Museum, **Cambridge.**
University Museum of Classical Archaeology, **Cambridge.**
Cheltenham Borough Council Art Gallery and Museum Service, **Cheltenham.**
Royal Scottish Museum, **Edinburgh.**
City Museum, **Leeds.**
City Museum, **Liverpool.**
British Museum, **London.**
Greek Museum, University of Newcastle, **Newcastle-upon-Tyne.**
Ashmolean Museum, **Oxford.**
Museum of Greek Archaeology, University of Reading, Whiteknights, **Reading.**

United States

John Hopkins Archaeological Collection, **Baltimore,** Maryland.
Walters Art Gallery, **Baltimore,** Maryland.
Palestine Institute Museum, Pacific School of Religion, **Berkeley,** California.
Indiana University Art Museum, **Bloomington,** Indiana.
Museum of Fine Arts, **Boston,** Massachusetts.
Bowdoin College Museum of Art, **Brunswick,** Maine.
J. Paul Getty Museum, **Malibu,** California.
Isaac Delgado Museum of Art, **New Orleans,** Louisiana.
Metropolitan Museum of Art, **New York,** New York.
Pierpont Morgan Library, **New York,** New York.
Walter Baker Collection, **New York,** New York.
Chrysler Art Museum, **Provincetown,** Massachusetts.
Santa Barbara Museum of Art, **Santa Barbara,** California.
Dumbarton Oaks Foundation, **Washington D.C.**

Ancient Greek sites

On the mainland and islands of Greece and parts of Turkey, you can still see Ancient Greek ruins. Here are the names of some places with interesting sites to visit.

Greece

Aegina
Athens
Bassae
Corinth
Delos (island of Delos)
Delphi
Dodona
Eleusis
Epidauros
Knossos (island of Crete)
Mycenae
Olympia
Olynthos
Sounion
Thera (island of Santorini)

Turkey

Miletus
Ephesus
Pergamon
Priene

Ancient Greece Index

ANCIENT ROME

Ancient Rome Contents

This part of the book tells you what life was like in Ancient Rome. It is full of scenes, like the one above of a Roman dinner party, which have been carefully reconstructed from archaeological evidence and other historical sources.

Some of the scenes include reconstructions of buildings, such as villas, flats or temples. Many of these are based on buildings which are now in ruins. A few, like the Pantheon, a temple in Rome (shown above), have been preserved almost intact.

Sometimes, instead of a reconstructed scene, you will see a reproduction of a Roman painting, carving or mosaic, such as this one of street musicians. Mosaics are pictures made up of small pieces of coloured stone.

There are also detailed illustrations of things the Romans used, such as furniture, pottery, jewellery and weapons. Some are based on objects shown in paintings or described in books, but most show objects that have been found.

The two main periods of Roman history are the Republic and the Empire and you will come across these terms as you read this part of the book. To find out more about them, as well as the politicians, emperors and other people mentioned, turn to the "History of Ancient Rome" on pages 188-189.

Dates are followed by the letters BC or AD. BC stands for "Before Christ". AD stands for *Anno Domini*, Latin for "in the Year of Our Lord", meaning the number of years after the birth of Christ.

You may want to see some Roman remains or sites for yourself. On page 190, there is a list of Roman sites you can visit and museums with good Roman collections.

Although the book concentrates on the city of Rome itself, much of the information applies to the lives of people throughout the Roman Empire. To find out what territories this includes, see pages 186-187.

Introduction to Ancient Rome

The history of Ancient Rome dates back to about 750BC and covers over 1,000 years. It started as a collection of small villages on a group of seven hills near the River Tiber in what is now called Italy. The villages grew together into the magnificent city of Rome, which conquered the rest of Italy and eventually acquired a huge empire, covering most of Europe and parts of the Middle East and North Africa. The territories conquered by the Romans were known as provinces. This book refers mainly to life in Rome and the surrounding areas in the first two centuries AD.

The people of Rome

As you read this book, you will often come across people referred to as citizens and slaves. The people of Ancient Rome were divided into citizens, who had many legal, political and other privileges, and non-citizens, who did not. Citizens consisted of plebeians (the lowest rank), *equites* (businessmen) and patricians (noblemen). Some non-citizens were free born, others were slaves or freed men and women (former slaves). Many slaves were prisoners of war.

Slave

Freed man and woman

Free non-citizen from the provinces

Plebeian

Eques

Patrician

How we know about the Ancient Romans

Archaeologists have excavated the remains of Roman towns, villas and other buildings, which have provided information about the way the Romans lived.

In Rome itself, remains of many of the buildings have survived and these give us a general idea of the way the city looked in ancient times. This is the forum as it looks today.

Two sites which have been especially useful are the towns of Pompeii and Herculaneum. In 79AD the volcano Vesuvius erupted and they were both buried under a layer of ash. As a result, they have been preserved in good condition until the present day.

Paintings on the walls of some of the houses show portraits of the people, as well as scenes from everyday life and legends about Roman gods and goddesses.

Many of the works of Roman poets, authors and historians have survived in libraries. These give us detailed accounts of Roman life and important events in the history of Rome.

This chart shows you some of the most important dates in the history of Rome. You can find out more about Rome's history on pages 188-189.

753BC	Founding of Rome. Rome ruled by kings.
510BC	Expulsion of kings. Founding of the Republic.
281-201BC	Wars with Carthage.
214-146BC	Wars with Greece and conquest of Greece.
54BC	Caesar's invasion of Britain.
59-51BC	Conquest of Gaul (France).
49BC	Julius Caesar becomes dictator.
44BC	Murder of Julius Caesar.
31BC	Beginning of the Empire (or Imperial times) Augustus (Octavian) is first emperor.
43AD	Beginning of conquest of Britain.
286AD	Diocletian divides the empire.
324-337AD	Constantine reunites the empire.
410AD	Sack of Rome by the Goths.
476AD	Last western emperor is deposed.

City Life

Part of the wall has been cut away, so you can see inside.

One-roomed flats

Flat with several rooms.

Shops

Most people in Rome and other large cities lived in blocks of flats three or four storeys high. These were built round a central courtyard and usually had shops on the ground floor. People with money to invest sometimes built apartment blocks and rented them out. Rents were high, although some blocks were so badly constructed that they fell down within a few years.

In Rome, torch-carrying nightwatchmen patrolled the streets, to keep law and order and to check that buildings were securely locked.

Fire was a problem, as many people burned fires in open containers, called braziers. In 6AD, a police and fire-fighting force was set up, called the Cohortes Vigilum.

Water was carried in pipes from lakes and rivers to the towns. Aqueducts were built to carry the pipes across the countryside.

Most people got their drinking water from the public fountains in the streets and washed in the public baths.

People could pay to have pipes connected to take water to their homes. Some did this secretly to avoid paying.

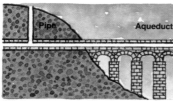

Many people used public lavatories, like these, though some apartments had their own lavatories on the ground floor.

The city's waste was carried in sewers under the streets. In Rome there was a huge sewer, called the Cloaca Maxima, which still exists today.

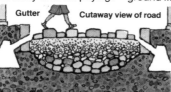

Pavements were raised up above the roads and there were stepping stones for pedestrians to use in wet weather. These also stopped carts from going too fast.

Many people had no kitchens of their own. They ate a lot of bread, which they bought from a public bakery.

Taverns and eating houses

People could also buy hot food and drink from eating houses and from stalls in the street. There were also taverns, where people went to drink wine and talk. Like the shops, these were often rooms, opening on to the street, on the ground floor of houses.

Shopping

Shop selling hot food   **Butcher**   **Shop selling cloth**   **Pottery shop**

Most Roman shops opened right on to the street, with a counter across the front. They were open early in the morning till late in the evening, with a long break in the afternoon.

Slaves were usually sent by their masters and mistresses to do the shopping for them. At night, wooden shutters were pulled across the shop fronts.

Shops selling olive oil were common, as it was used a lot both in cooking and for lamps. Some shops had their own olive press. The oil was stored in jars sunk in the ground.

The baker's shop usually had a mill at the back, where the flour was ground. The dough was made, then shaped into round, fairly flat loaves and baked in brick ovens.

To avoid traffic jams during the day, carts bringing goods to the market had to travel by night.

In Rome there were several markets, some specializing in a particular thing, such as meat or fish. In other towns, markets were held once a week in the forum, which was the centre of all business, political and legal activity in the town.

There were warehouses for storing goods. Some were built near the docks, so that boats could be unloaded easily.

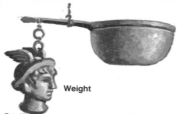

Weight

Stallholders used scales called steelyards. The amounts were marked off along the bar. You could tell how much something weighed by moving the weight along until it balanced.

There were inspectors, called *aediles,* who checked the quality of the goods at the market and tested the weights and measures to make sure they were accurate.

Near the forum were the more fashionable shops, selling luxuries, such as books, perfume, fine cloth and furniture.

Traders who could not afford a shop or market stall wandered the streets, carrying their wares over their shoulders.

If a Roman wanted to borrow money, he could go to a moneylender or a banker, who charged high rates of interest on the money they lent.

Money

The earliest kind of Roman money was a rough bar of copper or bronze with an ox or cow on it. The Latin word for money, *pecunia,* comes from *pecus,* the word for cattle.

The first type of round coin was called an *aes grave* and was made of bronze. On one side was the two-headed god, Janus, and on the other, a ship.

After 200BC, silver coins were brought in – the *denarius,* and later the *sestertius* (or ¼ *denarius*).

During the Empire, a gold coin, the *aureus,* came into use. Emperors usually had their portraits on coins. This one is Augustus.

Political events were sometimes recorded on coins. The two sides of this coin refer to the murder of Julius Caesar on the Ides of March.*

Military conquests and other achievements, such as the building of the Colosseum (above), often appeared on the reverse side of a coin.

*The Roman name for 15 March.

A Town House

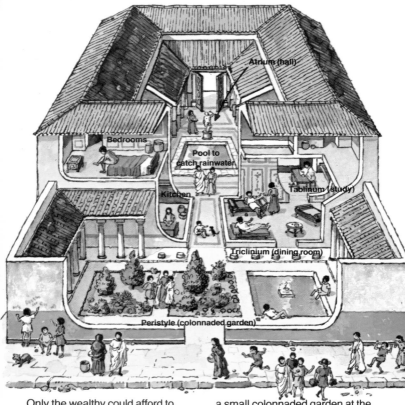

Atrium (hall)

Bedrooms

Pool to catch rainwater

Kitchen

Tablinum (study)

Triclinium (dining room)

Peristyle (colonnaded garden)

Only the wealthy could afford to have their own houses in the centre of the town. They were usually built to the same basic design, with a small colonnaded garden at the back. At the front of the house was the *atrium,* or hall, where guests were received.

Houses had door handles and knockers made of bronze. These came from a house in Pompeii.

Here are some Roman locks and keys. As a precaution against thieves, doors were heavy and were securely locked.

A·VE·CAN

Some houses had guard dogs too. "Beware of the dog" is the message on this mosaic, from Pompeii.

In the Kitchen

A rich man employed several cooks, each specializing in different dishes, and kept slaves to help them. Vegetables and sauces were cooked on wood or charcoal stoves and meat was roasted over an open fire. Most of the cooking was done in earthenware pots. They broke easily, but were cheap to replace.

Here are some Roman pots and cooking utensils. The tall jars, called *amphorae,* were used for storing wine and oil.

Wine was usually mixed with water, in a large bowl called a *crater,* before being served.

This cook is crushing spices and herbs in a mortar, using a club-shaped instrument called a pestle.

This bronze apparatus, rather like a tea urn, was used for keeping liquids warm (probably water or wine). The liquid went from the jar through a passage around the charcoal fire, and then out of the tap.

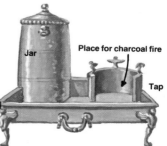

Jar

Place for charcoal fire

Tap

Eating

Poor people lived mainly on bread and a sort of porridge made of boiled wheat. Meat, fish and vegetables were expensive extras. Breakfast and lunch were both light meals. The main meal of the day was dinner. For wealthy people this sometimes lasted for several hours.

The Romans ate their food with their fingers, or with spoons. They did not use knives and forks.

Rich people had slaves to wipe their fingers clean for them between courses, using a bowl of water and a napkin.

A dinner party

In early times, men and women dined separately, but during the Empire, they were invited together. At dinner, the Romans lay on their sides on couches. Sometimes there were musicians and dancers to entertain the guests. It was also an occasion for poets and playwrights to come and read their latest works. Nine was considered the maximum number for a private party. Some Romans made it a habit to overeat and then make themselves sick, so as to have room to eat more.

Courses

Salad
Stuffed olives
Oysters
Dormice

The meal began with mixed hors d'oeuvres.

Ostrich
Lobster
Baby pig
Boar's head

The main course consisted of various meat and fish dishes.

Honey cakes
Stuffed dates

For dessert there were cakes made with honey, sweets, fruits and nuts.

Tableware

Here are some of the jugs, dishes and other things the Romans used at table. They were made of different materials – pottery, glass, bronze, silver or gold – depending on the wealth of the owner.

Dish

Ornamental vase

Bowl

Flask for wine or water

Bottle

Roman glass ranged from almost transparent colours to thick, opaque glass with white patterns on a coloured background.

Vase for storing oil

Cup

Goblet for drinking wine

Cup

Egg cup

Jug

Bowl

Dishes

Spoons

Jug

Bowl

Strainer

Every province had its own style of pottery. The most famous Roman pottery was Samian ware (above). Potters marked their goods, so we can trace where they were sold.

141

Furniture

Most ordinary flat-dwellers only had a few pieces of furniture, made of plain, rough wood. Furniture in more elegant houses was made of fine woods, bronze or marble and was often inlaid with silver, ivory, gold and tortoise-shell.

The Romans used chairs less than we do. They were kept mainly for women, old people or honoured guests. Instead, many people sat on stools, some of which could be folded. Some seats were upholstered and stuffed with wool.

Chests and cupboards were used for storing clothes and valuable objects.

The Romans ate from low, rectangular tables. Most houses also had small, ornamental tables, which were round or oval.

Statues and antique vases were displayed on tables or on special pedestals.

Couches were used at meals. They were high off the ground and often needed a stool to be reached.

Beds had leather or rope webbing, with a mattress of straw or wool. On top were blankets, a pillow and a bedspread.

Lamps

Roman houses were lit by oil-burning lamps. The oil was usually made from olives, nuts, fish or sesame seeds. Most lamps were made of pottery, but the more expensive ones were made of bronze and were very decorative.

Some lamps had small stands of their own, like this.

There were lanterns too, which were made to be hung from the ceiling.

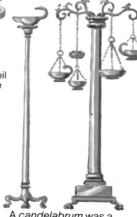

A *candelabrum* was a tall stand for putting a lamp on. Some had branches, so that several lamps could be hung from them at once.

Heating

To keep their houses warm, people used braziers, like these, which burned charcoal.

Central heating

For those who could afford to have one, there was a central heating system, called a hypocaust. The floors of the houses were raised on pillars. A fire was kept burning in the cellar and the hot air passed between the pillars and heated the rooms above.

143

Clothes

Most Roman clothes were made of wool or linen, although cotton and silk were also worn. Men always wore white for official or formal occasions, keeping bright colours for parties.

A man's basic clothing was a loincloth and a tunic. If he were a citizen, he would also wear a toga – a large piece of cloth wrapped round the body.

Togas

Toga for parties **Senator's toga** **Toga for mourning** **Emperor's toga**

Togas were normally white, but other colours were also worn. There were brightly coloured togas for parties and special occasions and dark togas for mourning. A senator's toga had a purple band and the emperor's toga was purple with gold embroidery.

Women's clothes

Clothing for women consisted of two pieces of underwear, an under tunic, with or without sleeves, and a dress, called a *stola*. A shawl, or *palla*, was sometimes worn on top.

Underwear **Tunic** **Stola** **Palla**

A *stola* for wearing at parties was often embroidered or decorated round the hem.

Outdoors, respectable women wrapped themselves up well, keeping their heads covered.

Children's clothes

Children were dressed just like adults. A rich boy wore a *toga praetexta,* which had a narrow purple band.

144

For travelling, people wore cloaks of various designs.

Here is a selection of different styles of Roman sandals, shoes and boots. They were usually made of leather.

Jewellery

Rings were the most common item of jewellery. They were worn by both men and women.

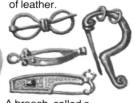

A brooch, called a *fibula,* was used for fastening cloaks and tunics. Some looked very much like safety pins.

Cameos were used in a lot of jewellery. They are semi-precious stones with faces or figures carved in them.

Roman women wore gold chains and necklaces. They used a wide range of precious and semi-precious stones, but the most prized were pearls, opals and emeralds. Diamonds were not used as they were too hard to cut.

Here is a selection of styles of Roman bracelets. The snake design was popular and had been used earlier by the Greeks.

Most Roman women had pierced ears so they could wear earrings. The ones on the right consist of tiny beads threaded in bunches.

145

Hair and Beauty

In the early days of the Republic, men kept their hair and beards in short, simple styles. Later, beards went out of fashion for a time.

During the Empire, some young men wore their hair fairly long and kept it oiled and curled. Beards were also shaped in elaborate styles.

Rich men had their own slaves to cut their hair and shave them, but most ordinary men went to a barber's shop. This was also a place to meet friends and hear the latest gossip.

The Romans had several cures for baldness, some of which had very unpleasant ingredients. Some men preferred to wear wigs instead.

Women's hairstyles

In the early Republic, women usually wore their hair in a simple bun. By the beginning of the Empire, many new styles were worn, with plaits, curls and waves. Heated tongs were used to make the hair curl. Here is a selection of some of the styles.

Strips of cloth were sometimes used to keep the hairstyles in place. Wealthy women had jewelled circlets and diadems too.

Hair pins were also used. Some were made of carved ivory or gold and were worn as hair ornaments.

For a time it was fashionable to have fair or red hair. Some women dyed their hair or had wigs made from the hair of foreign slaves.

Roman women plucked their eyebrows with tweezers. Hair was rubbed off the rest of the body with a pumice stone.

Some people had ivory false teeth fitted, like these. The Romans brushed their teeth with a special powder, rather like ground chalk.

This girl is pouring perfume into a flask. Roman men and women both used a lot of perfume, made from flowers, spices and scented woods.

Women used face packs to keep their skin soft and free of wrinkles. One Roman face pack was made of flour and ass's milk.

Powder jar   Spatulas

Perfume flask

Mirrors

Nail cleaner

Comb

Here is a selection of things a Roman noblewoman would have had on her dressing table. These mirrors are silver.

Here some slave girls are preparing their mistress for a party. Chalk is used as a face powder. Rouge is put on her cheeks, and her lips and nails are painted red. Her eyelashes and eyebrows are darkened and eyeliner is used. Roman make-up was made from vegetable and mineral dyes.

147

Growing up in Ancient Rome

In the early days, young children were brought up by their mothers. The girls were taught things like cooking and spinning.

From the age of seven, boys went out with their fathers to learn how to be farmers, craftsmen or soldiers.

Boys from well-off families were taught to read and write. They were trained for business or for an official career.

Later, wealthy women tended to hand over the care of their children to nurses and slaves.

When they were older, these children often had a private tutor, usually a Greek, to teach them.

Going to school

Although some children were educated at home, many others went to school – usually at about six or seven. They were taught reading, writing and simple arithmetic. Teachers were often strict and children were beaten if they did not learn their lessons.

Wax tablet

Styli

Abacus

Ink-well

Papyrus

Pens

Young children wrote on wax tablets with a hard stylus. Mistakes could be rubbed out easily. The older ones wrote on papyrus, a kind of paper made from papyrus reeds. They used ink, and pens made of reed or metal. An abacus was used to help with doing sums.

148

At the age of twelve, very bright boys and ones from wealthy families went to a secondary school, where they were taught by a *grammaticus*. They studied Greek, history, geography, arithmetic and the works of famous authors.

If a young man wanted a political or legal career, he also had to learn oratory, the art of speaking in public.

To help students and schools, libraries were set up by the state or by rich men.

Keeping fit was an important part of Roman education, to prepare boys for the army. After lessons, they were expected to take part in sports, including running, wrestling and fencing.

Games and toys

School started early in the morning and finished in the afternoon. Then, children were free to go to the baths or play games. Games included rolling hoops and knucklebones, which was played rather like jacks.

Sometimes children pretended to be charioteers. They raced in small carts led by donkeys.

Dolls and model figures, like these, have been found in children's graves.

149

The Baths

There were public baths through the empire, but the ones in Rome were magnificently decorated with marble and statues. Many citizens spent much of the day at the baths, as they were free or cost very little. The baths were not just places to wash.

They had gymnasiums and gardens, and often shops and libraries too. People went there to meet their friends and talk. There were usually separate baths for men and women, although mixed bathing was allowed at one time.

First, you went to the changing rooms, where you left your clothes on a shelf. There was always a risk someone might take them.

Before bathing, people often took some sort of exercise, such as wrestling or weight-lifting.

The hottest room was the *laconicum*. Hot air passed under the floor and inside the walls. A vat of boiling water made the room steamy.

The *caldarium* was another hot, steaming room, which made people sweat a lot. It had a pool with hot water for bathing in.

There was a furnace in the basement to heat the water. Slaves stoked the fire constantly to keep it hot. The water passed from the tank to the baths in lead or clay pipes.

Oil flask — Oil pan

Strigils

Instead of soap, the Romans rubbed oil on their bodies and then scraped it off with a stick called a *strigil.*

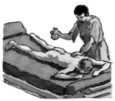

Some people took their slaves to the baths to do this for them, or hired a bath attendant.

After the hot bath, people often relaxed in the warm pool, called the *tepidarium.*

The cold bath, the *frigidarium,* was a large swimming pool – usually in the open-air. After a cold swim, you could relax by the poolside. For those who were hungry, there were often snacks for sale.

After the bath

For an extra fee, you could hire a trained attendant to give you a massage.

Barbers and hairdressers were often available. Slaves could be hired to provide beauty treatments.

For those with more serious interests, there were organized lectures and discussion groups.

There were gardens attached to the baths, where you could walk or meet your friends. For businessmen it was useful to find a quiet spot to discuss deals in private.

A large public baths might have had a library attached to it, so that people could study.

151

The Games

The Games was the name given to the fights and massacres that were held to entertain the Roman citizens. The idea began in 264BC, when two men staged a fight to the death between six slaves, as an offering to their dead father. Fights like this became very popular. They took place on public holidays, in honour of a god or a military victory.

At first the audience watched from wooden stands, but later stone amphitheatres, like the Colosseum in Rome, were built. They were equipped with lavatories and eating houses. The Games always began with a procession. The gladiators (the men who fought) were accompanied by dancers, musicians, jugglers, and priests.

Gladiators were slaves, criminals or men who were in debt. They were trained in special schools, often by former gladiators.

To make the fights more interesting, there were different styles of fighting with different weapons and armour. The two gladiators on the right are dressed as a Samnite and a Thracian, enemies of the Romans. The man with a net and trident was called a *retiarius*.

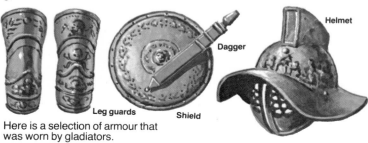

Helmet

Dagger

Leg guards

Shield

Here is a selection of armour that was worn by gladiators.

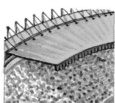

An awning, called a *velarium,* could be spread over the seating area, to protect the spectators from sun and rain.

Before the start of a fight, the gladiators greeted the emperor with the words, "Hail Caesar*, those about to die salute you".

The crowd decided the fate of a defeated man by praising or booing him. The emperor then signalled thumb up "let him live" or thumb down "kill him".

Successful gladiators became heroes and were rewarded with gold. If a gladiator won many fights, he might be able to buy his freedom.

Some gladiators were made to fight blindfolded on horseback.

Others were matched against wild animals, such as lions or tigers.

One of the most spectacular fights involved flooding the arena in order to reconstruct a naval battle, such as the one between the Athenians and the Persians.

Animals were imported from abroad and displayed in the arena. On one occasion herds of giraffe and ostriches were let loose, only to be hunted down by teams of archers.

Sometimes wild animals were set to fight each other to death.

On occasions, massacres were held in which Jews, Christians and criminals were killed by wild animals in the arena.

At the end of the fights the dead bodies were removed and sand spread everywhere, to cover the blood.

*Caesar was one of the emperor's titles.

153

Music, Dancing and the Theatre

Professional musicians and dancers performed at private parties, in theatres and before sporting events, such as racing or the Games. They were usually slaves or freed men and women.

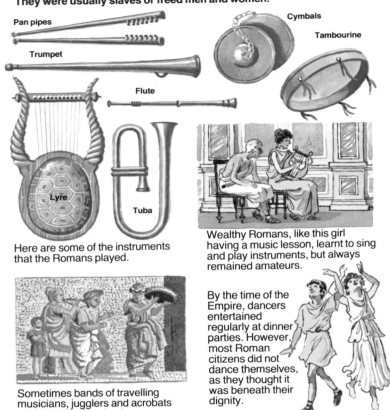

Pan pipes

Trumpet

Cymbals

Tambourine

Flute

Lyre

Tuba

Here are some of the instruments that the Romans played.

Wealthy Romans, like this girl having a music lesson, learnt to sing and play instruments, but always remained amateurs.

Sometimes bands of travelling musicians, jugglers and acrobats performed in the streets.

By the time of the Empire, dancers entertained regularly at dinner parties. However, most Roman citizens did not dance themselves, as they thought it was beneath their dignity.

The theatre in Rome dated from 240BC, when they began performing versions of serious Greek plays. However, Roman audiences preferred comedies.

The actors always wore masks, to indicate the kind of character they were playing.

154

Orchestra

At first, plays were performed on temporary wooden stages. From the 1st century BC, permanent stone theatres were built. They were based on Greek theatres, although the seats were supported on a series of arches and vaults, instead of being cut into the slope of a hillside. Important people sat in wide seats at the front. There was a curtain drawn across the stage until the beginning of the performance.

Most of the actors were freed men. Here a group of actors are dressing for a play. At first only men were allowed on stage, so they acted the women's parts.

Some actors became very popular and received "star" treatment from fans.

In later tragic plays, the words were spoken by the chorus, a group of men who stood in the orchestra. The actors mimed. This kind of actor was called a *pantomimus*.

In comedies there were changes too. The actors stopped wearing masks and women were allowed on the stage.

Sports and Games

The Romans were generally more interested in watching sports than in taking part, but they believed in keeping fit. Each town had an exercise ground, called a *palaestra*, usually attached to the baths. Men practised running, jumping, wrestling and javelin-throwing.

Professional athletes were usually Greeks. They could be recognized by their hair, which was tied in a knot on top.

Boxers fought wearing *caestus,* spiked gloves that could inflict terrible wounds on the opponent.

The Romans played various kinds of ball games. Some people had special rooms in their villas for ball games.

In the countryside, Roman nobles sometimes went hunting wild boar or deer. Hunting dogs, like these, were imported from Britain.

Fishing was another popular sport. People fished along the river outside Rome, using a simple rod and line or a hand-net.

Romans played a lot of gambling games with dice, and board games using counters. These dice are made of ivory.

Knucklebones had originally been a Greek game. It was played with four pieces – bones or bone-shaped bits of glass, pottery or bronze. The pieces had numbers on each side. The player threw the pieces and then scored as we do with dice.

Chariot Racing

Chariot racing was popular all over the empire. In Rome there was an enormous stadium called the Circus Maximus, which held 250,000 people. The charioteers were usually slaves or freed men. The reins were tied round their waists, but they carried knives so that they could cut themselves free if they crashed. They wore helmets for protection. The charioteers were divided into four teams – the Reds, Blues, Greens, and Whites. The spectators bet on which would win.

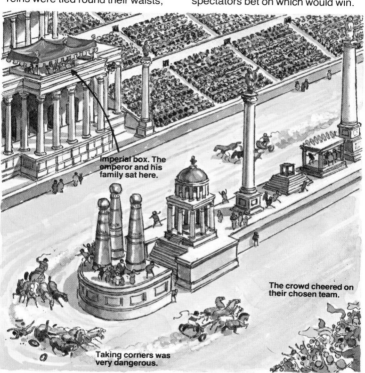

Imperial box. The emperor and his family sat here.

The crowd cheered on their chosen team.

Taking corners was very dangerous.

The race was usually seven laps of the course. Bumping and ramming were allowed and added greatly to the excitement and danger.

The winner was awarded a purse of gold and treated as a hero.

Villas and Gardens

During the 1st century BC, it became the custom for wealthy Romans to build themselves magnificent villas on their country estates, or at fashionable seaside resorts. The villas were usually one or two storeys high and had large, beautifully laid out gardens, with fountains and pools.

This Roman painting gives us some idea of what a seaside villa would have looked like.

The gardens were decorated with sculptures and vases. This boy on a dolphin was part of a sculpture for a fountain.

The walls inside the villas were brightly painted, often with landscapes or scenes from stories of gods and heroes.

The floors were paved or covered with mosaics . The designs ranged from geometric patterns to scenes with animals or people.

159

Farming

In early times, most Romans were farmers, but by the end of the Republic, most farming was done on large estates with slave labour. People with small farms and no slaves were unable to compete. This is a villa on a fairly large estate. The most important crops were cereals, grapes and olives.

Growing wheat and barley

Before sowing seeds, the land had to be ploughed. Roman ploughs were made of wood tipped with iron.

Then the seeds were scattered over the ground. Wheat and barley were the two main cereals grown.

When harvest time came, the crops were cut with a sickle. Then the stubble was burnt and the fields ploughed again.

In Gaul (Roman France), a cart with knives in front was invented to cut the wheat.

Threshing – separating the grain from the straw – was done by driving horses round the threshing floor.

Then the grain was winnowed – separated from the chaff – and stored in sacks in barns on the farm.

Fruit and vegetables

Grapes were grown for fruit and wine. They were grown on trellises, picked and loaded into baskets, to be taken back to the farm.

To make wine, the grapes were put into a stone trough and then trodden in to extract the juice. The men held poles to stop slipping.

A press was used to squeeze out the last drops of juice. The juice was stored in jars, where it fermented and turned into wine.

Olives were grown in many parts of the empire. The oil was used for cooking, lighting and cleaning.

The Romans also grew fruit trees. This man is grafting a branch from one tree to another, to improve the quality.

Market gardens outside Rome kept the city supplied with vegetables, herbs, fruit and flowers.

Meat and fish

Farmers kept chickens, geese and ducks for their eggs and for meat.

Cattle, sheep, pigs and goats were all kept for eating. The milk from cows and goats was drunk or made into cheese. Cattle hides were used for leather. Here a farm worker is milking a goat.

Some estates had fish ponds, which were well stocked with freshwater fish for the table.

Hunting was another way of getting food. The Romans hunted deer, boar, hares, partridges, pheasants and pigeons.

Paying rent

Some farmers had no land of their own, so they rented it from wealthy landowners. They paid in money, crops or animals.

People's Jobs

In the early days of Rome, most citizens worked for themselves as farmers, craftsmen, traders or labourers. By the end of the Republic, many of these jobs were done by slaves. Many of the poorer citizens, or plebeians, were out of work. For the nobles, only jobs in the government, the army or looking after their estates were considered respectable ones. Most women worked in the home.

In Rome, each trade had its own club, or *collegia,* which held meetings and dinners. The members paid money into a fund, to pay for things such as their own funeral expenses.

A lot of people, mostly slaves, were employed in mills, grinding grain to make flour. The mills were usually attached to bakeries. In some mills the grinding was done by donkeys.

By the 1st century AD, the Romans knew how to use water wheels to drive mill stones, but they were rarely used.

Metalsmiths made tools, weapons and household goods, using bronze, iron and copper. Jewellers made brooches, rings and other ornaments, using gold and silver.

Early glass-makers moulded the glass into shape. By the 1st century BC, the Romans were using the technique of glass-blowing, which they had learnt in the Near East.

Carpenters were employed in many trades, including building and furniture-making. Many of their tools looked like the ones carpenters use today.

Boat-building was a trade that employed many slaves.

Potters made the containers for cooking, serving and storing food. Some estates had their own potters.

Cobblers made a whole range of footwear, from heavy nailed boots for the army to slippers and sandals.

The job of spinning and weaving cloth was mostly done by women at home.

Finishing off new woollen cloth was done by fullers. First the cloth was soaked in urine to thicken it.

To clean the cloth, it was trodden in a mixture of sodium carbonate and fuller's earth, a kind of clay. People also sent their togas to the fullers to be cleaned.

The cloth was then hung on frames over sulphur-burning fires, to bleach it. The fumes were poisonous and some fullers caught serious lung diseases.

After being washed, the cloth was combed with teasels or hedgehog skins. The fluff produced was used to stuff pillows.

The cloth was hung out to dry, then folded and flattened in a large press.

Slaves were not employed only as labourers. Educated slaves often had clerical jobs. Some former slaves worked in government service.

Some trusted slaves became business agents for their masters. In their spare time they could conduct deals of their own, and make money to buy their freedom with.*

*See page 170.

163

Building

The stone for building was cut from quarries, usually owned by the state. Large numbers of slaves were employed to cut and lift the stone. Cranes were used to lift the larger ones. Stone blocks were removed from the quarry wall by drilling holes and filling them with wooden wedges. The wedges were then soaked with water, causing them to swell and split the stone. It was sometimes sawn into smaller blocks.

With huge supplies of slave labour, the Romans were able to tackle many building projects. They built new towns, forts, bridges and aqueducts, many of which are still standing today. Cranes and scaffolding were used to raise the stone into place.

Arches and vaults

To build an arch, an arch-shaped wooden support was put at the top of two columns of stone. Wedge-shaped stones were placed in position around the support.

To build a vaulted ceiling, this process was repeated all the way along the passage.

Materials

Many houses and flats were built from wooden frames filled with stones and mortar, a kind of cement, and a layer of plaster on top.

The mortar, which dried as hard as concrete, was made by mixing lime, sand, water and gravel.

Bricks were often used in building. Roman bricks were thinner than ours. They were made of clay, shaped in wooden moulds and baked hard in a kiln.

Decoration

The walls of elegant houses were decorated with paintings, or murals. The artist applied the paint while the plaster was still wet.

Public buildings and private villas were adorned with marble statues and busts. Sculptors and stone masons were hired to make them.

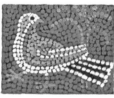

Floors were sometimes decorated with mosaics, pictures of patterns made from small pieces of coloured stone.

The mosaic maker worked from a plan. First he spread wet plaster over a small area of the floor and smoothed it down.

Then he pressed the pieces of stone into the plaster, making sure he followed the design on his plan.

Building a bridge

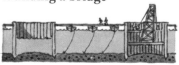

First a temporary bridge was set up across a row of boats. Wooden stakes, chained together in a circle, were driven into the river bed. The water was then pumped out of this enclosed area.

The area inside the stakes was filled with blocks of stone, which made the piers to support the bridge. When the piers were high enough, a wooden framework was hoisted into place between them.

Religion and Beliefs

For most people, religious life was based in the home. Each house had a shrine. Family ceremonies were held there and daily prayers were said to Vesta, goddess of the hearth.

In the shrine were figures of the Lares and Penates, spirits that guarded the family and the home.

Temples

This is what a Roman temple looked like. Each temple was dedicated to the worship of a particular god or goddess, whose statue was kept inside. The temples did not hold religious services with a congregation participating.

Outside the temple was an altar, where sacrifices of animals were offered to the gods on holy days.

People visited the temple of their favourite god or goddess if they had a special problem or favour to ask.

In order to please the god they might burn incense, say prayers or make an offering of money or goods.

Priests and priestesses served in the temples. They were in charge of receiving people's offerings and making sacrifices to the gods.

The chief of all the priests in Rome was the Pontifex Maximus. From the time of the Emperor Augustus (left), this position was always held by the emperor himself.

The temple of Vesta

There were some round temples, like the temple of the goddess Vesta, the most sacred shrine in Rome. A fire was kept burning inside by the Vestal Virgins, who were in charge of the shrine.

Every five years, a new girl was chosen to be a Vestal Virgin and she served for 30 years. She was forbidden to marry, but was highly respected and had special privileges.

Fortune telling

The Sibyl was a priestess who lived in a cave and foretold the future. The Sibyl's predictions were written down and consulted in times of trouble by emperors and politicians.

Augurs were priests who interpreted thunder and the flight patterns of certain birds, to tell whether the gods were pleased or angry with their worshippers.

A priest called a *haruspex* gained similar information by examining the liver of a sacrificed animal.

Special sacred chickens were kept. If they ate greedily, it was a good omen. Bad appetites meant that the gods were angry.

The Romans also believed that events were foretold in the stars. Many emperors kept an astrologer to advise them.

Ordinary people often went to fortune tellers who told the future with special dice, or by going into trances.

Curing illness

People who were ill sometimes sought a miracle cure by sleeping in the temple of the god of medicine, Aesculapius.

Others tried bathing in sacred springs, wells or baths.

Festivals

The Romans had a lot of public holidays, or holy days, usually to celebrate the festival of a god or goddess. Great processions were held. Animals, paid for by the government, were sacrificed at the altar outside the temple. Festivals were also occasions for feasting and drinking and visits to the Games.

New Year was celebrated on 1 March. Fresh laurel leaves were hung on the doors of buildings and the Vestal Virgins lit a new fire in their temple.

One of the liveliest festivals was Saturnalia, the feast of the god Saturn, which was held in December. Slaves swapped roles with their masters and were waited on.

The Lupercalia, in February, celebrated the founding of Rome. This statue shows the legendary founder, Romulus, and his brother, Remus, who were nursed by a wolf.

The festival of Flora, goddess of flowers, lasted for a whole week. Tables were piled high with flowers and people danced around wearing garlands of petals.

Family Customs

In early times, a father could order that a weak or deformed baby be left outside to die. This was because he could not afford to bring up a child who would not be able to work or fight. Later this was stopped, though fathers still controlled their children's lives and chose their husbands and wives.

On the 8th or 9th day of its life, a child was purified, named and given a *bulla,* a charm of gold or leather.

When a boy reached manhood, there was a day of celebration. He put on the grown-up toga and dedicated his *bulla* at the shrine.

Weddings

A wedding began with a sacrifice and then the bride and groom ate a special cake. There was a procession in which the bride was led by children to her new home, where her husband was waiting to greet her. After more ceremonies, she was carried over the threshold.

Women's lives

In early times, Roman women had few rights but many duties. A woman was always in the power of a man, first her father, then her husband, and then, if she became a widow, her son. Divorce was forbidden. Later, things improved and women gained more control over their own lives .

Funerals

When a rich person died, they were dressed in their best clothes and laid in the *atrium* of the house. Friends and relations came to pay their respects. On the day of the funeral, a procession took the body to the forum. Then people made speeches about the dead person.

The corpse was burnt on a fire and the ashes were placed in a jar called an urn.

The urn was placed in a family tomb, which was outside the city boundaries. Then everyone had a feast.

Many people's ashes were put in urns in huge underground tombs, called catacombs.

Slaves and Citizens

At the bottom of the Roman social scale were the slaves. They were completely at the mercy of their owners. Those with some skills, or who worked as private servants for kind owners, could lead quite reasonable lives. However, many others worked as labourers in conditions which were so bad that they died young of overwork. Sometimes slaves tried to run away, but they were usually caught.

In the early days, there were few slaves and they were usually treated as part of the family. As the Roman Empire grew, thousands of conquered people were taken and sold at slave markets.

Slaves were sometimes given tips, which they could save to buy their freedom. Some masters gave away freedom to their favourite slaves.

When a slave was freed there was a special ceremony, called manumission. Some slaves were freed in their master's will.

Many freed men and women worked hard and did well for themselves as traders or craftsmen. Some were made citizens.

Citizens

Citizens had many privileges which were denied to non-citizens. Non-citizens did not have access to many of the facilities in Rome, such as the baths or the Games. Citizens were entitled to wear the toga, a mark of social status. Yet, many of the lowest rank, the plebeians, were poor and unemployed.

The government paid a "dole" of free grain and provided baths, races and the Games, to keep the unemployed citizens quiet and happy.

The next rank of citizen, the *equites,* had once been cavalry officers. During the Empire, most were rich businessmen.

The richest and noblest Roman families were the patricians. Only they could hold the highest government offices.

Rich Romans increased their prestige by a system of patronage. Poorer citizens became clients, visiting the patron regularly and receiving money, clothes and perhaps the offer of a job. In return, clients supported their patrons in elections or in court cases.

The Government

In Republican times, the Romans were ruled by a group of men called the Senate, who were chosen from the patrician class. Government officials were elected by all male citizens. In Imperial times, the emperor had power over the Senate, and appointed the officials.

The Senate was made up of 300 (later 600) men, called senators. They decided on government policies and how public money should be spent. Here a meeting of the senators is in progress.

The letters SPQR were written on military standards. They stand for "the Senate and the people of Rome".

The plebeians had their own assembly, where they could accept or reject the proposals of the Senate. After 287BC, their own proposals, *plebescita*, had the force of law.

The plebeians elected tribunes to look after their interests. Later, emperors took the title of tribune.

A political career

A well-born young man who wanted a career in the government usually began with a few years in the army.

His first official appointment was likely to be that of *quaestor*, a government official dealing with finance.

The next step was to become an aedile, supervising markets, public buildings and the Games.

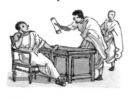

After that he might become a *praetor*, supervising law courts and making sure the laws were kept.

The highest postition was consul. The senators elected two consuls each year, to rule over the Senate.

An ex-consul could become a proconsul, governor of a province of the empire. Proconsuls were assisted by legates.

Professions and Learning

The Romans did not regard all professions equally highly. Teachers, for example, were looked down on and badly paid. Teaching was often done by Greeks. The Romans liked education to have a practical use. Lawyers were highly respected and law was considered a suitable training for a young man going into politics. Most authors and poets earned very little and depended on rich patrons, unless they had money of their own.

This is Virgil, one of the few well-paid Roman poets. He was author of the Aeneid, the story of the Trojan hero, Aeneas, and the founding of Rome.

A skill that the Romans regarded very highly was the art of oratory, or public speaking. It was essential for a political or legal career. This is the famous orator, Cicero.

Philosophers were also respected. People read their works and visited them to hear their teachings.

As printing had not been invented, books had to be written by hand. Booksellers employed slaves, usually Greeks, who could read and write, to do this.

Books were made by joining together sheets of papyrus – a kind of paper made from papyrus reeds. A stick was attached at one end and the papyrus was wound into a scroll, called a volumen. Later, books more like our own were made from sheets of vellum or parchment (both made from animal skin) folded and sewn together. This kind of book was called a codex.

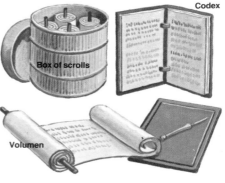

Box of scrolls

Codex

Volumen

Law

Roman law was based on the "Law of the 12 Tablets", which had been drawn up in the 5th century BC, laying down punishments for basic crimes. Later, new rules were added to cover issues that had not been dealt with. Some laws were adapted from those of subject peoples of the empire. In the eyes of the law people were divided into *honestiores* (honourables), who were well off, and *humiliores* (dishonourables), who were poor. *Humiliores* usually got much harder punishments.

An accused man could defend himself in court or pay a professional lawyer to act for him.

Medicine

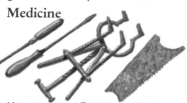

Here are some Roman surgical instruments. There were many skilled surgeons, but operations were risky, as there were no anaesthetics or antiseptics.

In early Rome there were no doctors. People tried to cure their families with home-made potions and traditional remedies. In the 2nd century BC, Greek doctors started coming to Rome and were paid well for their services. Besides medicines, they recommended balanced diets, fresh air, exercise, baths and massage. However, some doctors still tried to cure people with potions made from things like animal dung or gladiator's blood.

Numbers

These are the Roman numbers. When a number comes before one larger than itself, you subtract it, e.g. IV=4 (5−1). When a smaller number follows a larger one, you add, e.g. VII=7 (5+1+1).

I 1	II 2	III 3	IV 4	V 5
VI 6	VII 7	VIII 8	IX 9	X 10
XI 11	XII 12	XIII 13	XIV 14	XV 15
XVI 16	XVII 17	XVIII 18	XIX 19	XX 20
XL 40	L 50	XC 90	C 100	CC 200
CD 400	D 500	DC 600	CM 900	M 1000

The calendar

The Roman year began on 1 March, until 153BC, when it was altered to 1 January. The year was divided into 12 months, named after gods, emperors and numbers. The names we use are based on theirs. For example, March is named after Mars, July, after Julius Caesar and August after the Emperor Augustus. The year was 365 days long, but because they did not have leap years it started to get out of line with the seasons. Caesar corrected this in 45BC and in Britain it was not corrected again until 1752AD. The letters a.m. and p.m. stand for the Latin words *ante meridiem* and *post meridiem,* meaning before and after midday.

The Army

Almost constant warfare against their neighbours made the Romans experienced, efficient soldiers. In the early days, all property-owning citizens were expected to serve in the army, each providing his own weapons. Campaigns were usually held in the summer.

Hastatus or princeps   **Triarius**   **Veles**

The early armies had four kinds of soldiers. *Hastati* and *principes* were the younger, lighter-armed men. *Triarii* were older and more heavily armed. *Velites* were poor citizens with weapons but no armour.

Marius's reforms

Later, as the empire grew and much of the fighting took place abroad, a full-time professional army was needed. In the 2nd century BC the army was reformed by General Marius (left). He issued uniforms and weapons to all soldiers, and raised the pay.

Recruits were given rigorous training, which included marching, riding, swimming, fighting and building camps.

Dagger

Stabbing sword

Shield

Light pilum   **Helmet**

Chain mail shirt

Heavy pilum

Later, the chain mail shirts were replaced by armour made of segmented metal plates. In cold climates, the soldiers could wear breeches too.

Each soldier had a short stabbing sword, a dagger, a heavy and a light *pilum* (or javelin), a helmet, a shirt of chain mail and a shield. Each cohort (see next page) had a different coloured shield.

Senior officers had special made-to-measure armour made of moulded leather or bronze. This is Julius Caesar in his army uniform.

The organization of the army

The army was divided into legions. By the time of the Empire, there were 28 legions, each divided into ten cohorts. The First Cohort was the largest and had 800 men. The other cohorts had 480 men, who were divided into six centuries of 80 men each. Ordinary soldiers were called legionaries.

Some legions had special names and emblems. This is the running boar, symbol of the 20th Legion, called the Valeria Victrix.

Each legion was commanded by a legate and had a standard with an eagle on top, carried by an aquilifer.

Beneath the legate, there were six officers called tribunes. The senior tribune commanded in the legate's absence. Tribunes were often young men starting a political career.

The prefect of the camp was the third in command, after the legate and the senior tribune. He was in charge of equipment and engineering works, such as building camps.

Each century was commanded by a centurion. Other officers included the trumpeter, the standard bearer and the centurion's deputy.

Trumpeter

Centurion

Standard bearer

A century was divided into groups of eight men who shared a tent and ate together. This group was called a *contubernium.*

A troop of cavalry was attached to each legion. They acted as scouts and carried messages in battle.

Non-citizens could become auxiliary soldiers, attached to a legion. After 25 years, they were given citizenship and their sons could become legionaries.

175

Going to war

When the army went on campaign, each soldier had to carry his own equipment. This included weapons, tools, bedding, cooking pots and enough food for three days.

Each night they built a camp by digging a ditch around the tents. The earth thrown up from the ditch formed a rampart, into which they planted wooden stakes.

Here a doctor is at work on the battlefield. Camps and forts had well-equipped hospitals for the sick and wounded. As well as soldiers, the legions had their own doctors, clerks, priests, engineers, surveyors and labourers.

Discipline in the army was strict. There were punishments laid down for each offence, ranging from extra work to flogging and death.

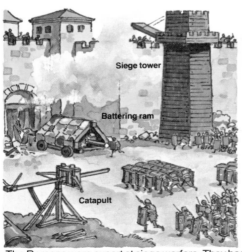

Siege tower

Battering ram

Catapult

Soldiers arranged their shields in a "tortoise" formation, like this, so that they could march safely towards the enemy.

The Romans were expert at siege warfare. They had catapults that could hurl heavy rocks and arrows at the enemy and battering rams to beat down enemy walls. Siege towers with drawbridges were used to climb on to the walls.

Although the soldiers were paid, taking booty was regarded as one of the rewards of capturing an enemy city or fort.

Defence

The Romans built permanent stone forts along their frontiers. Legions were posted there to guard the frontiers, keeping invaders out and maintaining law and order among the population.

The Emperor Hadrian built a great wall across the north of England, to defend the most northern part of the Roman Empire.

Ships

Roman warships ranged in size from biremes, which had two banks of oars, to quinquiremes, which had five. These ships were used mostly for transporting troops, though the Romans fought many sea battles with the Carthaginians of North Africa. Ships were also used to fight piracy.

The Empire

The Praetorian Guard were the emperor's bodyguards. They were paid well to ensure their loyalty.

There were several awards for bravery, such as medals and crowns. When soldiers retired they were given money or land.

After a victory, the emperor held a triumphal procession, or built an arch or column, to celebrate and to impress his subjects.

Travel and Transport

Travel throughout the empire was made easier by the excellent roads the Romans built. The roads were always straight, unless there was a serious obstacle, such as a mountain, in the way. This enabled the army to march swiftly to any trouble-spots. There were milestones every 1,000 paces. (A pace is equal to two steps and 1,000 paces is roughly 1,500m.)

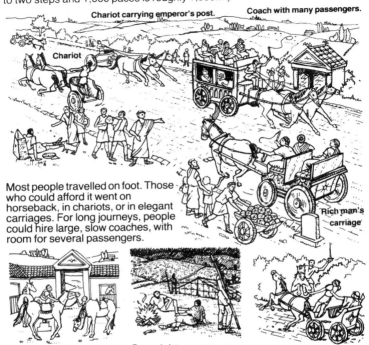

Chariot carrying emperor's post.

Coach with many passengers.

Chariot

Rich man's carriage

Most people travelled on foot. Those who could afford it went on horseback, in chariots, or in elegant carriages. For long journeys, people could hire large, slow coaches, with room for several passengers.

There were wayside inns, where travellers could stop and rest or change their horses.

Overnight, people set up tents by the roadside. Rich travellers brought servants and guards with them.

Bandits were a constant danger, despite the army's efforts to keep the roads safe.

Travel in Rome

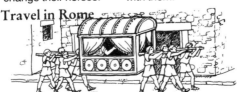

In Rome itself, wheeled vehicles were not allowed during the day, so the rich travelled in litters, carried by slaves. Some litters were made of rare woods, with fittings of gold, silver and ivory. Inside there were cushions and curtains.

Carts carrying heavy goods travelled by night. They were pulled by horses, mules or oxen.

178

Building a road

First, surveyors marked out the new road with stakes. They used an instrument called a *groma* (shown here), to make sure the land was level.

Then workmen dug a trench and laid stone kerbstones. Major roads were about 12m wide.

Cross-section

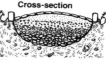

Firm foundations were built up from layers of sand, stone and pebbles. The top layer of stones was curved slightly, to drain off rainwater.

Sea travel

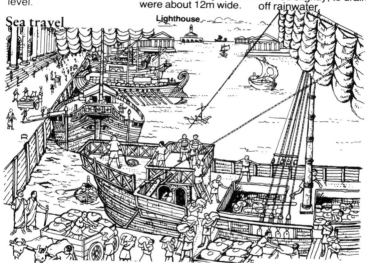

Lighthouse

The Romans traded with all parts of the empire and beyond. The goods travelled by sea, usually through the port of Ostia, on the coast near Rome. Pirates were a threat to shipping until patrolling warships, under General Pompey, got rid of them. By the time of the Emperor Augustus, about 120 ships sailed as far as India each year.

Heavy goods were often transported inland by river. Some river boats were towed, others could be sailed or rowed.

Some wealthy Romans were keen tourists and they visited places all over the empire, for their health, education or for a holiday.

179

Architecture

The Romans were very impressed by Greek architecture and borrowed not only Greek styles, but Greek architects and craftsmen too. For this reason, Roman architecture looks very similar to that of the Greeks.

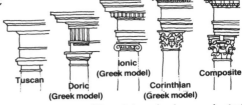

The Romans used five styles of column, adapted from the three that were used in Greek architecture. Columns were used for decoration as well as for support.

Roman temples looked very like Greek ones. They were mostly oblong with a triangular carved pediment and columns at the front. The temple was built on a platform, with steps leading up to it.

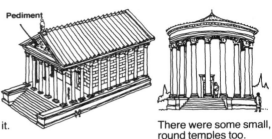

There were some small, round temples too.

Town planning

Whenever the Romans built new towns, they planned them on a grid, so that the streets were all at right angles or parallel to each other.

The basilica became the model for all the early Christian churches. It was usually rectangular, and had a central nave with a lower-roofed aisle on each side. The aisles were sometimes lined with columns.

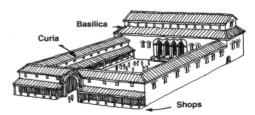

Each town had a forum, an open space where public meetings and markets could be held. Situated around the forum were shopping arcades, the curia (where the town council met), and the basilica (the law courts).

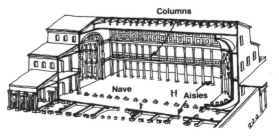

Arches, vaults and domes

Although the Romans did not invent the arch, they put it to greater use than anyone before them, building huge bridges and aqueducts all over the empire.

Triumphal arches, like this, were built in Rome and the provinces, to celebrate victories in battles.

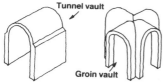

Tunnel vault

Groin vault

The tunnel or barrel vault was made simply by extending the arch, or building a series of arches, to make a tunnel shape. A groin vault was made by overlapping two tunnel vaults at right angles.

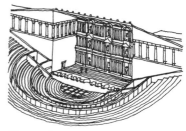

Roman theatres were built on flat ground and had arches and vaults to support the seats. In Greek theatres the seats had been built into the natural slopes of a hillside.

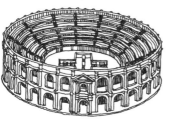

The Romans applied the same technique to building amphitheatres, the round and oval stadiums in which gladiator fights and chariot races were held.

Domes were a Roman invention. They were built by putting vaulting over a circular area. This is a cut-away view of the Pantheon, a Roman temple which is now used as a church.

Gods and Goddesses

Most Roman gods and goddesses closely resembled those of the Greeks, although they had different names. The Romans also adopted other gods, from the people they conquered. In Imperial times, it became the custom to worship emperors as gods as well. The Romans believed their gods and goddesses watched over every aspect of life, although, by the 1st century BC, many of the ruling classes had begun to lose faith in them.

◀**Juno** *(Hera),* Jupiter's wife, goddess of women and childbirth.

Minerva *(Athene),*▶ goddess of wisdom.

◀**Mars** *(Ares),* god of war.

Jupiter *(Zeus)**, ▲ god of thunder and king of all the gods.

Venus *(Aphrodite),* ▲ goddess of love and beauty.

Apollo *(Apollo)* god of the sun.▼

Neptune *(Poseidon),*▼ god of the sea.

Ceres *(Demeter),* goddess of corn.

Diana ▲ *(Artemis),* goddess of the moon and hunting.

Mercury *(Hermes),* messenger of the gods and patron of merchants. ▶

Faunus *(Pan)* and **Flora,** god and goddess of the countryside.▼

Bacchus *(Dionysus),* god of wine.

Dis Pater *(Hades)* and **Proserpine** *(Persephone),* god and goddess of the underworld.▼

The names in brackets are the Ancient Greek names.

Mystery cults and foreign gods

By the late Republic, some Romans had lost faith in the traditional gods and found little comfort in worshipping them. So they turned to new, foreign gods, whose cults often included secret rites and ceremonies, and promised eternal joy to their worshippers.

At first, many Romans regarded these new cults with great suspicion because they often took place in secret and involved wild celebrations.

Most cults, like that of the Egyptian goddess, **Isis** (above), promised life after death for its members.

Cybele, the mother goddess from Asia Minor, was the subject of another popular cult.

The Persian sun god, **Mithras,** was worshipped by many soldiers. Women could not join his cult.

The Romans usually allowed their conquered subjects to continue worshipping their own gods. This is the British goddess, **Epona.**

Another foreign goddess was **Diana of the Ephesians,** who was different from the Roman Diana.

Sometimes a local god merged with a Roman one, like **Sul-Minerva,** goddess of the sacred spring which provided the water at Bath.

Only a few religions were outlawed, among which was that of the Druids. The Romans disapproved of their custom of human sacrifice and their plots against Roman rule, and the Druid priesthood was destroyed.

Early Christians were persecuted, as they refused to worship the emperor and were regarded as a dangerous secret society. However, their numbers grew, and in 313AD the emperor made Christianity legal.

The City of Rome

Temple of Jupiter Stator

Colosseum

Aqueduct

Forum

Temple of Julius Caesar

Senate House

Arch of Severus

This is a reconstruction of part of the city of Rome, as it would have looked at the beginning of the 4th century AD. Many of the ruined buildings you can see today were built after the great fire of 64AD, in the reign of the Emperor Nero, which destroyed much of the city.

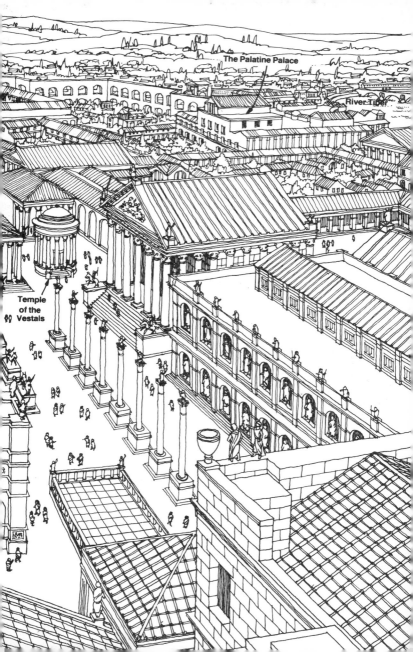

The Palatine Palace

River Tiber

Temple
of the
Vestals

The Roman Empire

This map shows the Roman Empire at the beginning of the 2nd century AD, when it was at its largest. The Romans began by conquering the territories around their city, in order to make it safe from enemy attack. They went on to conquer other countries and gradually built up a huge empire.

Towns, roads, bridges and aqueducts were built and trade links set up. The Romans extracted taxes from their subject peoples and established a common political and legal system. The Roman language, Latin, was spoken all over the empire. In 212AD, the Emperor Caracalla gave citizenship to all the subject peoples, except slaves. Before that people had had to earn the right to citizenship.

Later, the Roman Empire was threatened by the Persians, from the south east, and by barbarians from the north east. In the 4th century AD, barbarian tribes invaded. Eventually Rome itself was captured and the Empire destroyed.

The dotted line shows the boundaries of the empire at its largest.

The provinces of the empire were ruled by governors, called proconsuls, assisted by officials and troops. Some tried to make their fortunes by over-taxing the people and keeping the extra money.

Although many settled down peacefully under Roman rule, some, like Queen Boudicca of the Iceni tribe in Britain, resented their loss of independence and rebelled.

Black Sea

Ravenna

Neapolis
(Naples)

Athenae
(Athens)

Constantinople
(Istanbul)

Pergamum
Smyrna
Ephesus

Corinthus
(Corinth)

Antioch

Mediterranean Sea

Damascus

Leptis Magna

Cyrene

Alexandria

Jerusalem

EGYPT

Sometimes Roman rule clashed with the religious loyalties of people such as the Jews and Christians.

Legions were stationed at forts all over the empire, to deal with rebellions.

In Europe, North Africa and the Middle East today, you can still see Roman remains. This is the market-place at Leptis Magna in Libya.

The History of Ancient Rome

According to tradition, the history of Rome dates back to 753BC. A group of farmers built fortified villages near the River Tiber in Italy. These villages eventually grew together to make a city.

Legend has it that Rome was founded by a man named Romulus. Romulus and his twin brother, Remus, had been cast out to die by a wicked uncle, but were then saved and looked after by a wolf.

Rome was ruled by kings until 510BC. The last king, Tarquin the Proud, was so unpopular that he was expelled by the people. A republic was set up and two consuls were elected each year to rule.

At first the Romans were kept busy defending themselves against powerful neighbours. As they grew in numbers and strength, they conquered more and more land around them. By 250BC, the Romans ruled all Italy and were a powerful force in the Mediterranean area.

The Romans had to fight the Carthaginians of North Africa and the Greeks, who both saw Rome as a threat to their interests. Between 264 and 146BC there were three wars with the Carthaginians. Most of the battles took place at sea.

A young Carthaginian general, called Hannibal, set out from Spain with a huge army, which included 36 elephants. They crossed the Alps into Italy, but never succeeded in capturing Rome. In 146BC, the Romans finally destroyed Carthage.

Civil war broke out in Rome as rivals fought for political power. There were riots too, as the poor plebeians demonstrated against the rich patricians. In 73BC, a slave called Spartacus led 90,000 slaves into revolt. They succeeded in fighting off the army for two years.

Two political rivals, Caesar and Pompey, struggled for control of the government. Pompey was murdered and Caesar emerged as dictator in 46BC. In 44BC he was assassinated by Brutus, Cassius and others who feared he might try to make himself king.

More civil wars followed. Caesar's great-nephew, Octavian, became the first emperor (31BC - 14AD) and changed his name to Augustus. This is the beginning of the period known as the Empire.

Augustus's family ruled as emperors until 68AD, when there were four emperors in the same year. Then came a long period of prosperity and military success under such great emperors as Vespasian, Titus, Trajan, Hadrian and Marcus Aurelius (below). The empire continued to grow in size.

By the 3rd century AD, Rome began to have problems. Rival military leaders, backed by different factions in the army, struggled to become emperor. Prices rose and the empire became hard to govern. Barbarians from the north and the east began attacking the frontiers.

The Emperor Diocletian (284–305AD) tried to stop prices rising and keep back the barbarians. Christians were often blamed for the problems and many were put to death. To make governing easier, Diocletian split the empire, so there was one emperor for the east and another for the west.

The Emperor Constantine (306–337AD) made Christianity legal. He reunited the empire and built Constantinople as its new capital. At his death, the empire was divided once more. The Eastern Empire became known as the Byzantine Empire. In the west, whole provinces were overrun by barbarians and in 410AD, Rome itself was sacked.

The western emperor and his court had already fled to Ravenna for safety. In 476AD, the last western emperor was deposed. The Eastern Empire continued to be ruled from Constantinople, until 1453AD, when it was overrun by Turks.

Museums and Sites

Here are the names of some museums where you can find interesting collections of Ancient Roman objects.

Australia

Nicholson Museum of Antiquities at the University of Sydney, Sydney, **New South Wales.**

Canada

Museum of Fine Arts, Montreal, **Quebec.**
Royal Ontario Museum, University of Toronto, Toronto, **Ontario.**

United States

Metropolitan Museum of Art, New York City, **New York.**
Museum of Fine Arts, Boston **Massachusetts.**
University Museum, University of Pennsylvania, **Philadelphia.**
Museum of Art, Cleveland, **Ohio.**
Rhode Island School of Design, Museum of Art, Providence, **Rhode Island.**

United Kingdom

In Britain, you can still see the remains of many things that the Romans built, as well as collections of Roman objects in museums. The list below (arranged in alphabetical order of countries) includes some interesting sites as well as the best museum collections.

England:
Roman Baths and Roman Baths Museum, Bath, **Avon.**
Roman amphitheatre and Grosvenor Museum, Chester, **Cheshire.**
Tullie House Museum, Carlisle, **Cumbria.**
Dorset County Museum, Dorchester, **Dorset.**
Castle Museum, Colchester, **Essex.**
Corinium Museum, Cirencester, **Gloucestershire.**
City Museum, Gloucester, **Gloucestershire.**

Chedworth Roman Villa and Museum, Yanworth, **Gloucestershire.**
District Museum, Chichester, **Hampshire.**
City Museum, Winchester, **Hampshire.**
Verulamium Roman Town and Museum, St Albans, **Hertfordshire.**
Brading Roman Villa, Brading, **Isle of Wight.**
Lullingstone Villa, Eynsford, **Kent.**
Jewry Wall Museum and Site, Leicester, **Leicestershire.**
City and County Museum, Lincoln, **Lincolnshire.**
The British Museum, London.
Museum of London, London.
Hadrian's Wall, **Northumberland.** Not all the Wall is visible. The main sites are: Chesterholm Roman Fort and Settlement, Bardon Mill; Housesteads Museum and Site, Bardon Mill; The Clayton Collection, Chesters, nr Chollerford; Corbridge Roman Station, Corbridge; Temple of Mithras, Carrawburgh.
Aldborough Roman Museum, Aldborough, **North Yorkshire.**
Rowley's House Museum, Shrewsbury, **Shropshire.**
Museum of Antiquities, The University, Newcastle, **Tyne and Wear.**
Bignor Roman Villa, Bignor, **West Sussex.**
Fishbourne Roman Palace, Fishbourne, Chichester, **West Sussex.**

Wales:
Roman Amphitheatre and Legionary Museum, Caerleon, **Gwent.**
Caerwent Roman Site, Caerwent, **Gwent.**
Segontium Roman Fort Museum, Caernarfon, **Gwynedd.**
National Museum of Wales, Cardiff, **South Glamorgan.**

Scotland:
Antonine Wall remains can be seen at Rough Castle, nr Cumbernauld, **Strathclyde.**
Hunterian Museum, Glasgow University, Glasgow, **Strathclyde.**